Education and Information Technology Annual – 2013

A Selection of AACE Award Papers

Edited by

Theo J. Bastiaens, Ph.D.

Gary H. Marks, Ph.D.

Published by
AACE--Association for the Advancement of Computing in Education

Education and Information Annual - 2013
(ISBN # 978-1-939-797-00-1) (ISSN # 2168-8478) is published by
AACE, PO Box 1545, Chesapeake, VA 23327-1545, USA
757-366-5606; Fax: 703-997-8760; E-mail: info@aace.org
© Copyright 2013 by AACE
www.aace.org

Available at http://www.aace.org/bookshelf.htm

Introduction

The Association for the Advancement of Computing in Education (AACE),
http://AACE.org, founded in 1981, is an international, not-for-profit, educational
organization with the mission of advancing Information Technology in Education and E-
Learning research, development, learning, and its practical applications.

AACE serves the profession and community with international conferences, high quality
publications, leading-edge Digital Library (http://EdITLib.org), Career Center, and other
opportunities for professional growth.

We are proud to present to you this selection of 15 award winning papers from AACE's
conferences (http://AACE. org/conf). This year's selection includes papers from the
annual conference of the Society for Information Technology & Teacher Education
(SITE) in Austin (TX), World Conference on Educational Multimedia, Hypermedia and
Telecommunications (Ed-Media) in Denver (CO) and World Conference on E-Learning
in Corporate, Government, Healthcare, and Higher Education (E-Learn) in Montréal
(Canada). The decision to nominate a conference paper for an award was made by peer
reviewers. All authors were honored during the conference and received a certificate that
serves as testimony to their outstanding research and contribution to the conference.

This AACE book groups the award winning papers into four parts. These four parts
provide a timely overview and record of topics that are of primary interest in educational
technology this year.

We hope that the reader enjoys this selection as much as we enjoyed working with these
cutting-edge scholars. It is the second year that we publish this edition. We are grateful
for all the feedback and positive comments we received on the 2012 book. We look
forward to many future editions of AACE's award papers.

Thank you very much for your support and participation in AACE events and activities.

Theo J. Bastiaens

Gary H. Marks

Part 1
Theoretical Foundations, Systematic Approaches and adoption

In part 1 of this collection the focus is on papers that discussed the theoretical foundations behind educational technology. Many researchers are looking for a systematic approach when they develop software, implement a technology or create learning activities. In chapter 1, McGivern, Morgan et al. try to apply Socio-Cultural theory in combination with Distributed Cognition for the design of collaborative learning activities. They explain how Socio-Cultural theory and Distributed Cognition can provide significant insights into the educational utility of such collaborative technology and how design issues relating to collaborative learning may be addressed.

In chapter 2 online learning materials based on the cognitive theory of multimedia learning are the subjects of research. The authors, Ibrahim and Callaway, expect especially those online learning materials to improve student-learning outcomes. More specific, the authors examine the effect of online learning material designs on students' cognitive load and self-efficacy. Course designs (with and without segmentation), self-efficacy and the perceived difficulty of the content are also studied.

The following paper, in chapter 3, evaluates the effects of modality and multimedia comprehension on the performance of students with varied multimedia comprehension abilities when exposed to high complexity, self-paced multimedia instructional materials. The author, Al-Abbasi expects poor multimedia comprehenders to suffer from a decreased ability to comprehend complex textual and pictorial materials.

In chapter 4, the author Hopper, explains that digital portfolios, implemented in the learning process, can be an important tool for student growth. A digital collection of student work across disciplines promotes reflection, self-evaluation, goal setting, and feedback. Effective implementation requires that students know how to think critically and reason well. However systematic methods of teaching critical thinking are not always provided in schools, leaving gaps in the effectiveness of a digital portfolio. She shows us that teaching a growth mindset to students before using digital portfolios transforms an instrument for student growth into a growth mindset tool.

Part 2

The Teacher, the Curriculum and Technology

In chapter 5 , Matusiak reports the findings of a case study that examines the use of digital information resources in an undergraduate geography class. The study assumes a contextual approach and focuses on the use of visual and multimedia resources in specific class contexts.

Chapter 6 addresses the affective human experiences in terms of the emotions of South African teacher-students while attaining computer competencies for teaching and learning, and for ODL. The authors, Esterhuizen, Blignaut et al. investigate how computers contribute towards affective experiences of disadvantaged teacher-students.

The next chapter provides an awareness of the evaluation of a large-scale nationwide ICT project in Australia. The Teaching Teachers for the Future project funded by the Australian Government has developed an evaluation plan using both quantitative and qualitative methods. The author, Albion, recounts some aspects of the development of the evaluation plan, describes the methods being used, and presents some insights from preliminary analysis of the data for one of the 39 teacher preparation institutions participating in the project.

Part 3 Social Media Opportunities

In part 3 of this collection we start with the impact of using Facebook as a social learning platform. In chapter 8 the authors Yamauchi, Fujimoti et al. examine the so-called "Socla study program" to build a social learning community for high school students using Facebook and other Internet services. In this program the students worked on individual study projects that focused on their future plans. The authors investigated how the program was accepted by the students and how it affected their views on the future.
The authors in chapter 9, Weber and Rothe, report on the findings of a study conducted on the use of the social networking service NING in a cross-location e-learning setting named "Net Economy". They describe the implementation and value of the implemented social networking service with regard to the need for a social presence, as emphasized by the Community of Inquiry framework.
Chapter 10 covers the importance of science, technology, and society within the social studies classroom. By using social network tools, students have the ability to refine their critical thinking skills and prompt social inquiry. Additionally, the authors Kilinc, Evans et al. will highlight how social networking tools are aligned with social studies curriculum. The chapter includes examples of lessons that teachers can use in the classroom, as well as connections to national and state social studies standards.

Part 4 New Phenomena in Learning: Virtual Realities, Robotics and agents

In part 4 new phenomena in learning are introduced. Chapter 11 explores how Augmented Reality using mobile phones can enhance teaching and learning in education. It specifically examines its application in two cases, where it is identified that the agility of mobile devices and the ability to overlay context specific resources offers opportunities to enhance learning that would not otherwise exist. The author Latif considers the technologies that will be used to develop these resources, along with logistical issues surrounding affordability, security and safety issues of mobile devices.
In chapter 12, the authors Frerichs, Barker, et al. explain Geospatial and Robotics Technologies for the 21st Century. These technologies teach science, technology, engineering and mathematics (STEM) through robotics, global positioning systems (GPS), and geographic information systems (GIS) activities. So participants use a robotics kit, handheld GPS devices, and GIS technology to explore STEM related careers. The hybrid learning experience that the project has created brings together an on-line curriculum, digital manipulatives and real-world experiences.

Chapter 13 describes the potential of socially-oriented pedagogical agent and interactive simulation in e-learning system. The authors Ballera and Elssaedi investigate the impact of a socially oriented tutor agent with the incorporation of interactive simulation in e-learning. Results on student performances, -perceptions and -experiences in computer science are reported.

The next chapter identifies and examines how virtual simulations function to train pre-service teachers learning to conduct individualized education program team meetings. Pre-service special education teachers enroll in a mild/moderate distance degree and licensure program. The authors, Mason, Glomb et al. examine the specific behaviors emitted by each participant throughout simulated meetings, as well as the antecedent stimuli and consequences controlling these behaviors.

The final chapter 15 explains the development and use of an online English collocations on demand system as help for Japanese researchers to acquire a good command of English collocations. To make actual collocation problems clear, the authors Ohtake, Fujita et al. compared collocation patterns used by Japanese researchers with those used by native speakers of English. For this purpose, they compiled a learner corpus consisting of about 10,000,000 words taken from papers published by Japanese researchers.

TABLE OF CONTENTS

AUTHORS AND EDITORS CONTACT INFORMATION

Chapter 1. Learning Theory for Collaborative Large Shared Digital Spaces
Daniela McGivern, Michael Morgan and Matthew ButlerMonash, University
E-mail: daniela.mcgivern@monash.edu

Chapter 2. Assessing the Correlations Among Cognitive Overload,
Online Course Design and Student Self-efficacy
Mohamed Ibrahim, Rebecca A. Callaway, Arkansas Tech University
E-mail: mibrahim1@atu.edu

Chapter 3. The Effects of Modality and Multimedia Comprehension on the Performance of
Students with Varied Multimedia Comprehension Abilities when exposed to High
Complexity, Self-paced multimedia Instructional Materials
Daniah Al-Abbasi, Texas Tech University
E-mail: daniah1@yahoo.com

Chapter 4. Digital Portfolio Use as a Growth Mindset Tool
Susan Hopper, University of North Texas
E-mail: susanhopper@my.unt.edu

Chapter 5. Use of Visual and Multimedia Resources in an Undergraduate Classroom: A Case
Study
Krystyna K. Matusiak, University of Denver
E-mail: krystyna.matusiak@du.edu

Chapter 6. Computer Literacy Learning Emotions of ODL Teacher-Students
Hendrik D. Esterhuizen, A. Seugnet Blignaut, Christo J. Els & Suria M. Ellis
North-West University, South Africa
E-mail: Hennie.Esterhuizen@nwu.ac.za

Chapter 7. Looking for evidence of change: Evaluation in the Teaching Teachers for the
Future project
Peter R. Albion, University of Southern Queensland, Australia
E-mail: Peter.Albion@usq.edu.au

Chapter 8. Impact of Using Facebook as a Social Learning Platform to Connect High School
Students with Working Adults
Yuhei Yamauchi, Toru Fujimoto, Kaoru Takahashi Junko Araki Yusuke Otsuji Hisashi
Suzuki, The University of Tokyo, Sanno University, Benesse Corporation, Japan
E-mail: yamauchi@iii.u-tokyo.ac.jp

Chapter 9. Social Networking Services in E-Learning
Peter Weber, Hannes Rothe
South Westphalia University of Applied Sciences, Germany
E-mail: weber.peter@fh-swf.de

Editors

Theo J. Bastiaens is professor of Educational Technology at the Fernuniversität in Hagen, Germany and part time professor at the Open University, The Netherlands. He is a member of the AACE board of directors. •E-mail: Theo.Bastiaens@fernuni-hagen.de

Gary H. Marks is CEO and founder of AACE-Association for the Advancement of Computing in Education (http://AACE.org) and CEO of SITE-Society for Information Technology in Teacher Education (http://SITE.aace.org). E-mail: info@aace.org

Association for the Advancement of Computing in Education

CELEBRATING 30+ YEARS OF SERVICE TO THE IT IN EDUCATION/E-LEARNING COMMUNITY

Invitation to Join

The Association for the Advancement of Computing in Education (AACE) is an international, non-profit educational organization. The Association's purpose is to advance the knowledge, theory, and quality of teaching and learning at all levels with information technology.

This purpose is accomplished through the encouragement of scholarly inquiry related to technology in education and the dissemination of research results and their applications through AACE sponsored publications, conferences, and other opportunities for professional growth.

AACE members have the opportunity to participate in topical and regional divisions/societies/ chapters, high quality peer-reviewed publications, and conferences.

Join with fellow professionals from around the world to share knowledge and ideas on research, development, and applications in information technology and education. AACE's membership includes researchers, developers, and practitioners in schools, colleges, and universities; administrators, policy decision-makers, professional trainers, adult educators, and other specialists in education, industry, and government with an interest in advancing knowledge and learning with information technology in education.

Membership Benefit Highlights

• Gain professional recognition by participating in AACE sponsored international conferences

• Enhance your knowledge and professional skills through interaction
  with colleagues from around the world

• Learn from colleagues' research and studies by receiving AACE's
  well-respected journals and books

• Receive a subscription to the Professional Member periodical
  AACE Journal [electronic]

• Receive discounts on multiple journal subscriptions,
  conference registration fees, and EdITLib Subscriptions.

• Access EdITLib-Education & Information Technology Digital
  Library, a valuable online resource that is fully searchable
  and covers 30+ years of academic journals and international
  conference proceedings.

• AACE Social Networking http://aace.org/networking
  Connect with Colleagues Worldwide!

 **AACE Blog:**
http://blog.aace.org

 **AACE Facebook:**
http://facebook.com/aaceorg

 **AACE Twitter:**
http://twitter.com/aace

www.aace.org

AACE Journals

Abstracts for all journal issues are available at www.EdITLib.org

Education & Information Technology Digital Library – Electronic

The EdITLib is your source for peer-reviewed, published articles (40,000+) and papers on the latest research, developments, and applications related to all aspects of Educational Technology and E-Learning. Included are 1,000s of articles from AACE journals and international proceedings.

International Journal on E-Learning

(Corporate, Government, Healthcare, & Higher Education)
(IJEL)   ISSN# 1537-245   Quarterly

IJEL serves as a forum to facilitate the international exchange of information on the current theory, research, development, and practice of E-Learning in education and training. This journal is designed for researchers, developers and practitioners in schools, colleges, and universities, administrators, policy decision-makers, professional trainers, adult educators, and other specialists in education, industry, and government.

Journal of Educational Multimedia & Hypermedia

(JEMH)   ISSN# 1055-8896   Quarterly

Designed to provide a multidisciplinary forum to present and discuss research, development and applications of multimedia and hypermedia in education. The main goal of the Journal is to contribute to the advancement of the theory and practice of learning and teaching using these powerful and promising technological tools that allow the integration of images, sound, text, and data.

Journal of Interactive Learning Research

(JILR)   ISSN# 1093-023X   Quarterly

The Journal's published papers relate to the underlying theory, design, implementation, effectiveness, and impact on education and training of the following interactive learning environments: authoring systems, CALL, assessment systems, CBT, computer-mediated communications, collaborative learning, distributed learning environments, performance support systems, multimedia systems, simulations and games, intelligent agents on the Internet, intelligent tutoring systems, micro-worlds, and virtual reality-based learning systems.

Journal of Technology and Teacher Education

(JTATE)   ISSN# 1059-7069   Quarterly

A forum for the exchange of knowledge about the use of information technology in teacher education. Journal content covers preservice and inservice teacher education, graduate programs in areas such as curriculum and instruction, educational administration, staff development, instructional technology, and educational computing.

Journal of Computers in Mathematics & Science Teaching

(JCMST)   ISSN# 0731-9258   Quarterly

JCMST is the only periodical devoted specifically to using information technology in the teaching of mathematics and science. The Journal offers an in-depth forum for the exchange of information in the fields of science, mathematics, and computer science.

CITE – Electronic Journal

CITE — CONTEMPORARY ISSUES IN TECHNOLOGY & TEACHER EDUCATION

An electronic publication of the Society for Information Technology and Teacher Education (SITE), established as a multimedia, interactive electronic counterpart of the Journal of Technology and Teacher Education.

Association for the Advancement of Computing in Education

aace.org/pubs • pubs@aace.org

AACE MEMBERSHIP

Membership Options

AACE MEMBERSHIP

- Subscription to 1 AACE print Journal (see below)
- Full online access to back issues of that journal
- Online subscription to the AACE Journal
- Discounted conference registrations and proceedings
- Discount subscriptions to additional journals
- Access to the AACE Career Center and Job Board
- All the benefits of AACE Membership.

US $125 Non-US $145

- All the same benefits of a Professional Membership
- Offered at a discount for students
- MUST be enrolled as a full-time student in an accredited educational institution and provide school information below

US $45 Non-US $65

The *Only* Digital Library Dedicated to Education & Information Technology

- All the same benefits of a Professional Membership
- PLUS 1-year subscription to the EdITLib with thousands of peer-reviewed journal articles, conference papers and presentations, videos, webinars and much more

$175

The *Only* Digital Library Dedicated to Education & Information Technology

- All the same benefits of a Professional Membership
- PLUS 1-year subscription to the EdITLib
- Offered at a discount for students
- MUST be enrolled as a full-time student in an accredited educational institution and provide school information below

$75

New Option!

- Registration as a virtual participant for the following events:
  EdMedia – World Conference on EdMedia & Technology (Value $225)
  E-Learn – World Conference on E-Learning in Corp. Govt., Health, & Higher Ed. (Value $225)
  Global TIME – Global Conference on Technology, Innovation, Media & Education (Value $225)
  Global Learn – Global Conference on Learning & Technology (Value $225)

- **Full access** to EdITLib - The Only Digital Library Dedicated to Education & Information Technology (Value $150)
- **Conference proceedings** for AACE events, accessible in EdITLib – Education and Information Technology Digital Library
- **AACE F2F Conference Registration discounts**

$395
(Value $1,050)

- Libraries may purchase subscription to AACE print Journal(s) and/or the EdITLib

❑ International Journal on E-Learning (IJEL)	$195
❑ Journal of Educational Multimedia and Hypermedia (JEMH)	$195
❑ Journal of Computers in Math and Science Teaching (JCMST)	$195
❑ Journal of Interactive Learning Research (JILR)	$195
❑ Journal of Technology and Teacher Education (JTATE)	$195
❑ EdITLib – Education & Information Tech. Library (electronic)	$1795

Additional shipping charge of $15 per journal per year for non-U.S. addresses

- **Professional & Student Memberships** include a subscription to 1 AACE print Journal *(not included in virtual membership)*
- Additional journals can be added to your membership

- Please choose ONE option:

❑ Add 1 Journal $115 prof / $35 student
❑ Add 2 Journals $150 prof / $60 student
❑ Add 3 Journals $205 prof / $85 student
❑ Add 4 Journals $260 prof / $110 student
❑ Add 5 Journals $315 prof / $135 student

Additional shipping charge of $15 per journal per year for non-U.S. addresses

Applicant Information

Name: _____   E-mail: _____

Address: _____   City: _____ State: _____

Postal Code: _____ Country: _____ ☐ New Member ☐ Renewal Membership # _____

If applying as a student please provide **School/Institution Name:** _____ **Expected Graduation Date:** _____

Select Journal(s) to receive: (*Membership includes 1 journal. See above for adding addit.*) ☐ IJEL ☐ JEMH ☐ JCMST ☐ JILR ☐ JTATE

Method of Payment (US Dollars)

Enclosed: ❑ Check (U.S. funds & bank, payable to AACE) ❑ Purchase Order *(PO must be included plus $10 service charge)*
❑ Bank Wire *(Wire info must be included plus $25 service charge)*

Credit Card: ❑ MasterCard ❑ VISA ❑ AMEX ❑ Discover

Card # _____ Card Exp. Date ___/___ Signature: _____

TOTAL:
$ _____

AACE 2013 Conferences

Details for conferences are available at **www.aace.org/conf**

The exchange of ideas and experiences is essential to the advancement of the field and the professional growth of AACE members. AACE sponsors conferences each year where members learn about research, developments, and applications in their fields, have an opportunity to participate in papers, panels, poster demonstrations and workshops, and meet invited speakers.

24ᵀᴴ INTERNATIONAL CONFERENCE SOCIETY FOR INFORMATION TECHNOLOGY AND TEACHER EDUCATION

March 25-29, 2013
New Orleans, Louisiana, USA

This conference, held annually, offers opportunities to share ideas and expertise on all topics related to the use of information technology in teacher education and instruction about information technology for all disciplines in preservice, in-service and graduate teacher education.

EdMedia 2013

World Conference On Educational Media & Technology

June 24-28, 2013
Victoria, British Columbia, Canada

This annual conference serves as a multi-disciplinary forum for the discussion of the latest research, developments and applications of multimedia, hypermedia and telecommunications for all levels of education.

E-Learn 2013

World Conference on E-Learning in Corporate, Government, Healthcare, & Higher Education

October 21-25, 2013
Las Vegas, Nevada, USA

E-Learn is a respected, international conference enabling E-Learning researchers and practitioners in corporate, government, healthcare and higher education to exchange information on research, developments and applications.

Global Learn 2013

Global Conference on Learning and Technology

November 6-7, 2013
An Online Conference

This annual conference serves to further the advancement and innovation in learning and technology. As the educational world becomes increasingly global, new ways to explore, learn, and share knowledge are needed. Global Learn is a means to connect and engage creative educators, researchers, consultants, training managers, policy makers, curriculum developers, entrepreneurs, and others in the topics and fields in which they are passionate. Global Learn offers an opportunity to meet and discuss their ideas, findings, and next steps.

Association for the Advancement of Computing in Education

www.aace.org

1 Learning Theory for Collaborative Large Shared Digital Spaces

Daniela McGivern, Michael Morgan and Matthew Butler

Background

Interactive tabletop technology has developed considerably over the past decade, with research charting their evolution and use (Dillenbourg & Evans, 2011, Higgins, et. al. 2011, Khandelwal & Mazalek, 2007, Piper et al. 2006, Piper & Hollan, 2009). In recent years increases in the size of this technology has facilitated the creation of large shared digital spaces, and with this, the ability to create collaborative face-to-face digital learning spaces. Such a hardware platform was discussed in Morgan and Butler (2009), in which a low-cost large format multi-touch display was described. Of particular interest, however, is how collaborative applications can be designed for such a platform. Traditional notions of human computer interaction can be challenged when users surround the surface, and consideration of how to get users to interact and collaborate effectively is of the utmost importance. Interface design and interaction considerations have been explored in previously reported work (Butler et. al. 2010, McGivern et. al. 2011) focusing on the context of a Phonics literacy application designed for primary school children.

Preliminary reporting suggested how learning task analysis could be used, with initial data collection suggesting that this was a successful approach to application design for the large shared digital spaces. There is a need, however, to more closely consider the theoretical underpinnings of learning applications on the technology to strengthen the collaborative interactions that can take place on large shared digital learning spaces.

Fig 1: Technology for a Large Shared Digital Space.

Theoretical Issues

This paper argues that the design of collaborative learning environments involving large shared digital spaces can be conceptualised by using Socio-Cultural theory and Distributed Cognition/Activity theory as a base to explore a number of important educational issues. Social interactions can demonstrate robust learning effects and it is important to understand the mechanisms for collaborative learning using Socio-Cultural Theory (Vygotsky, 1978, Wertsch, 1985) to explain how people relate to each other in an interactive social context. Distributed Cognition/Activity theory (Engeström, 2001, Hutchins, 1995, Jonassen & Reeves, 1996, Nardi, 1996, Turner & McKewan, 2004), which is an extension of Socio-Cultural theory, examines how individuals interact in their environment through the use of tools, resources and materials thereby producing a cognitive system that involves aspects of the social context (Hollan, Hutchins, & Kirsh, 2000). Large shared digital spaces are a particular kind of mediating artefact and it is important that the interface elements and interactions designed into such learning environments are carefully considered.

Unlike individual theories of learning (Anderson, 2000, Terry, 2009), Vygotsky theorised that learning also occurs when individuals share information and through this interaction they construct an understanding together that could not be achieved alone (Eggen & Kauchak, 2007). This is the basis of Socio-Cultural learning theory (Vygotsky, 1978, Wertsch, 1985). Parents, teachers and older children, play an important role in the learning of young children as they provide the cognitive tools for development and support, particularly with regard to support for the acquisition and use of language. Wertsch (1985) has studied Vygotsky's theoretical approach and states that there are three core themes that form an interdependent framework. These are (1) a reliance on a genetic, or developmental, analysis; (2) the claim that higher mental processes in the individual derive from social life; and (3) the claim that human action, on both the social and individual planes, can be understood only if we understand the tools and signs that mediate them (pp. 14-15).

The sociocultural principle puts forward the approach that development relating to how children learn is 'interpersonal'. It begins on a social level, externally, and then is 'intrapersonal', moving to an individual internal level. Vygotsky (1978) states that in the process of internalisation a number of transformations occur:

(a) An operation that initially represents an external activity is reconstructed and begins to occur internally.
(b) An interpersonal process is transformed into an intrapersonal one. Every function in the child's cultural development appears twice, first on the social level, and later, on the individual level. First, *between* people (*interpsychological*), and then *inside* the child (*intrapsychological*). All the higher functions originate as actual relations between human individuals.
(c) The transformation of an interpersonal process into an intrapersonal one is the result of a long series of developmental events (pp. 56-57).

Therefore, social interaction plays an important role in a child's cognitive development that begins through external social activity, which is then eventually internalised. These same principles can be applied to present-day learning environments through the use of new educational tools such as large shared digital spaces. Large shared digital spaces can create an interpersonal learning and development environment that through two processes, social activity and task breakdown, will enable individuals to finally internalise socially enacted shared understandings.

Vygotsky (1978) writes the zone of proximal development (ZDP) "...is the distance between the actual developmental level as determined by independent problem solving and the level of potential development as determined through problem solving under adult guidance or in collaboration with more capable peers" (p. 86). There are two limits to the ZPD, the lower limit that includes skills, tasks or abilities that a child is capable of achieving independently and requires no assistance and the upper limit that refers to tasks that are within a child's reach with some degree of assistance (Fox & Schirrmacher, 2011, p. 79; Hill, 2006, p. 5). This intervention involves an adult, teacher or peer assistant, who support and scaffold the child to solve their problem enabling them to achieve their goal and move to the next step. Wood, Bruner, and Ross (1976) state "...[t]his scaffolding consists essentially of the adult 'controlling' those elements of the task that are initially beyond the learner's capacity, thus permitting him to concentrate upon and complete only those elements that are within his range of competence" (p. 90). According to Brown (1992, p. 191) the ZPD can include adults as well, with many levels of expertise, and with a variety of tools such as books, videos, wall displays, scientific equipment, and computer environments providing learning support. This may include large shared digital spaces. The structure of such a collaborative learning environment can be considered to be an interpersonal representation of the learning task, and to some extent the thought process required to manage the learning task. Support is provided to learners via a social learning environment and interaction with one or more peers.

Like the ZPD, if pieces of information are divided and distributed between a group's members, the group problem solving would be more effective than just that of an individual (Hatano & Inagaki, 1991). According to Hatano and Inagaki (1991, p. 334) humans naturally seek to understand and are more likely to search for meaning when problem solving in a group environment. A group will bring to the table, per se, a "richer data base" as "...no individual member has acquired or has access to all needed pieces of information, but every piece is owned by at least one member in the group" (Hatano & Inagaki, 1991, p. 335). The ZPD provides the setting in which the social and the individual are brought together through speech and mediation (Daniels, 2001, pp. 8-9). A large shared digital space can be considered to be the mediation point, the peer assistant that is the ZPD, which scaffolds and guides the learner by means of creating an interactive, collaborative learning environment. These learning environment processes can be designed to scaffold learning by dividing tasks into individual components and making the learners conscious of rules and methods by which the interaction is to be conducted. As reported in Butler et. al. (2010) "The key to this process is to make each learner aware of his or her specific role, its place in the overall activity and to provide the appropriate tools for them to complete the sub-task." (Butler et. al. 2010, p. 1445). Therefore, the learning task is represented firstly explicitly as interpersonal interactions, as a set of roles, tools and tasks, which via reflection can become implicit and intrapersonal. The division of tasks ensures that learners discuss concepts and interact verbally.

During the latter part of the 1920's, Vygotsky's main focus was on the use of tools or instruments to control behaviour (see Fig 2) , known as an "instrumental act," of "a unit of activity mediated by signs" (Daniels, 2005, p. 33). It was the use of these signs, tools, instruments or artificial stimuli, that was said to be unique to human beings, and considered to be the mediating point (see X in Fig 2) (Daniels, 2005, p. 33; Vygotsky, 1978, p. 39).

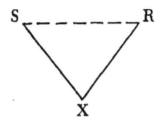

(Key: S = Stimulus, R=Response, X=Mediating Point).

Fig 2: Vygotsky's structure of sign operations (Vygotsky, 1978, p. 40)

Vygotsky's research demonstrated that humans use language, as a form of communication, as well as other developed sign systems, to stimulate and influence their own behaviour (Daniels, 2005, p. 33; Vygotsky, 1978, p. 39). Vygotsky wrote that "the central fact about our psychology is the fact of mediation " (Vygotsky, 1997, p. 138) and that higher forms of mental functioning are mediated by culturally derived artefacts, such as signs (Fernyhough, 2008). Vygotsky's sociocultural approach refers to human activities in a cultural context that are mediated by social processes and other symbol systems (John-Steiner & Mahn, 1996, p. 191).

It is these social processes and semiotic mechanisms, symbol systems or psychological tools, such as language that mediate social and individual functioning, that eventually leads to internalisation (Wertsch & Stone, 1986, pp. 163-164). These semiotic mechanisms provide the connection of the external with the internal and the social with the individual (Wertsch & Stone, 1986, p. 164). This aspect of Vygotsky's work has been developed and extended in the form of Distributed Cognition theory in order to describe the properties of cognitive systems involving many people and in particular cognitive systems involving designed artefacts.

An early proponent of Distributed Cognition theory, Hutchins (1995, p. 176) argued that an established culture or a society as a group, might have some cognitive properties and that may operate differently at the individual and group levels. Roberts in 1964, cited in Hutchins (1995, p. 177), suggested that the cultural group can be seen as a more widely distributed memory in terms of being collective memory, which is more robust and has a much greater capability that that of an individual's memory.

> "When computational tasks are socially distributed, there are two layers of organization to the activity: the computational organization, as defined by the computational dependencies among the various parts of the computation, and the social organization, which structures the interactions among the participants to the computation" (Hutchins, 1995, p. 185-186).

Large shared digital spaces are members of a class of cognitive tools that enhance "the cognitive powers of human beings during thinking, problem solving and learning" (Jonassen & Reeves, 1996, p. 693). A technology such as large shared digital spaces, where all learners can interact simultaneously through touching the screen, facilitates distributed cognition in a number of different ways. In effect the representation of the problem in the shared digital space stores and displays the current state and shared understanding of the problem, thereby allowing individuals to synchronize and coordinate their activity. The large size provides a shared digital space that enables us to create a face-to-face social learning environment where learners can share rich communications about the problem. In order to enable this shared activity, rich communication and shared manipulation of the problem, large shared digital spaces require a new interface paradigm in order to support effective human computer interactions in the context of multiple users and to facilitate the social learning organisation. Several specific issues associated with the design of interfaces for multi-user touch based applications have been described in Butler et. al.(2010):

> "Due to the fact that users directly manipulate objects on the screen with their fingers rather than using a mouse pointer it is important to consider how to represent objects and functions. To date our screen designs have focused on using icons and nested icon sets to represent functions rather than using menu systems. Providing icon sets for particular users may be one method of tracking specific users." (Butler et. al, 2010, p. 1445).

Questions of screen orientation and learner distribution around large shared digital spaces are dependent on the specifics of the learning interaction and so need to be carefully considered.

Leont'ev, a student of Vygotsky, extended Vygotsky's framework, by analysing human activity into three defined areas: activity, action and operation. Nardi (1996) describes Activity Theory as being complex whereby the unit of analysis, the activity, is dynamic and changes as conditions change and where all levels move up or down. Turner and McEwan (2004, p. 425) write that Leont'ev's idea should not be considered to be singular entities, but concentric layers with the *operations-conditions* level being the *how*, the *action-goal* level being the *what* and the *activity-motive* level being the *why*. This was eventually depicted as a triadic interaction between subject(s), which can consist of one or more people, and a group's object, its purpose, that is mediated by a tool or artefact. In brief, "…the subject carries out the activity, the artefact is any tool or representation used in that activity (internal or external to the subject), and the object encompasses both the purpose of the activity and its product or output" (Turner & McEwan, 2004, p. 426).

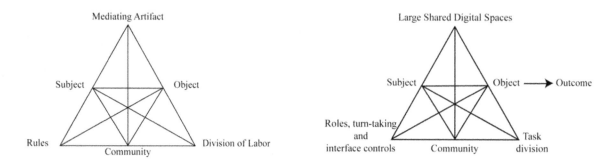

Fig 3: (a) Engeström's description of Activity theory (b) A Learning Activity System adapted from Engeström (2001, p. 136).

Leont'ev's theory was expanded even further in the 1980's by a Finnish academic, Yrjö Engeström (2001), who took the idea of Activity theory out of the classroom and into the workplace. Engeström's extended version included extra elements such as *community*, other group activity stakeholders, and the *division of labour*, the horizontal and vertical divisions that have responsibility and power within the activity. Finally *rules* are the formal or informal standards that govern the relationships between the subjects and the community (see Fig 3a) (Turner & McEwan, 2004).

However, Engeström's concept can also be applied to a learning activity system (see Fig 3b) where the elements are interwoven and associated with each other either directly or indirectly. Nardi (1996) states that the activity theory framework is composed of internal and external elements and are considered to be "fused, unified" (p. 76). It is internal to people as it involves specific objects and goals, and at the same time, external to people, as it involves artefacts, other people, and specific settings. The collaborative learning environment begins with the large shared digital space(s) that becomes the mediating artefact. The *subject(s)* are the learners, the participants. The *object* is the purpose, the learning activity, which produces the learning *outcome*. The *community* are the stakeholders, participants, who form the active group and on a wider scale, the classroom as a whole, who become the eventual group participants. The task division, *division of labour* that is shared between participants and encourages shared discussion in the activity (*object*). The roles, turn-taking, and interface controls govern the *rules* between the subjects, the *community,* who are actively participating in the activity, and the *object*. This also leads to group interaction, encourages conversation, that produces the learning outcome.

In conclusion, Socio-Cultural theory provides a rationale for the need for learning environments where a shared understanding of a problem can first be represented on an 'interpersonal' level for later internalisation as an 'intrapersonal' learning experience. Secondly, the importance of the concept of support to the learner in the ZPD through interactions with peers and careful interaction and interface design, is highlighted. In addition, the concept of mediation in Distributed Cognition/Activity theory provides an insight into how cognitive systems comprising one or more person and artefacts can coproduce learning outcomes that may be significantly different from individual learners.

Experimental Design and Research Instruments

An experimental treatment was implemented based on the content area of Phonics instruction for remedial learners (Fig. 4). The application was presented on a large shared digital space that allowed simultaneous touch-based interactions by up to four participants. The Phonics learning task was decomposed into two separate sub-tasks, **Phonemic awareness** (identifying and manipulating individual sounds and in spoken words) and **Phonics** (understanding the relationship between the sounds of spoken language, and the letters that represents those sounds) (U.S. Department of Education Office of Elementary and Secondary Education [USDOE], 2002). Each sub-task was designed to be assigned to a learner (on a rotating basis), who then needed to communicate with the other learner(s) in order to fill in missing letters in random word groups. Therefore the learners needed to collaborate in order to complete the main task. Figure 4 depicts a four learner version of the Phonics application that was developed.

The experimental design consisted of two phases (Fig 5). Phase One, used university students to conduct a usability analysis to examine the design principles, interface design, design usability, and human-computer interaction (HCI) of the phonics application. The Phase One participant pool for the study consisted of IT students from Monash University due to their expertise in interface design and usability issues. A survey instrument was constructed including a mix of Yes/No, Likert Scale and Open-Ended questions. Each section concluded with open-ended questions that enabled participants to raise any unknown issues. The survey consisted of a demographic section, 16 Likert scale questions and 15 short answer questions (see Fig. 6). Participants experienced 5-10 minutes of interaction with the application in pairs and then completed a 15-minute survey.

Fig 4: Phonics Application on a Large Scale Shared Digital Space

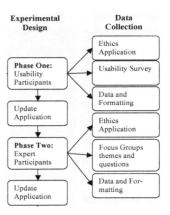

Fig 5: Experimental Design and Data Collection

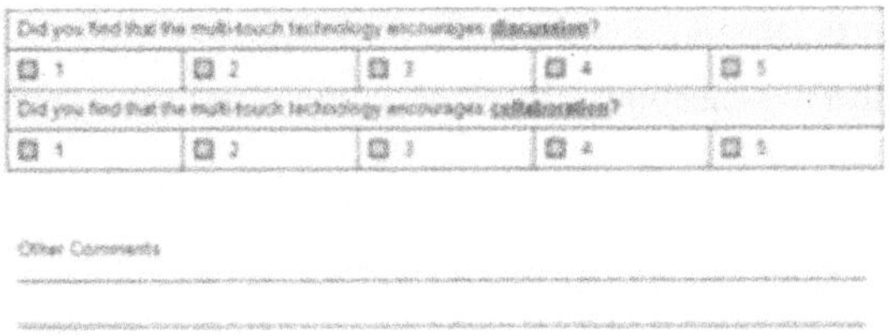

Fig 6: A Sample of the Likert Scale and Open-ended Questions in the Survey.

Phase Two, used experts to participate in focus group sessions to evaluate the learning and collaborative aspects of the large shared digital space. For Phase Two a potential pool of expert participants was identified as either: a) academics or teachers who had expertise in educational technology issues or; b) academics involved in early childhood studies or; c) a degree related to literacy instruction and being a literacy teacher with at least 2 years experience. Focus group sessions are described by Kumar (2005, p. 124) as exploring the perceptions, experiences and understandings of a group of people who have some experience in common with regard to a situation or event. Sharp, Rogers and Preece (2007) explain that the use of props, in this case a literacy application on a large shared digital space, provides context for the participants and helps to ground the data in a real setting. The focus group sessions provided this research with a richer and deeper explanation and exploration than a general survey. Focus group themes were developed in order to guide and focus the discussion (see Fig. 7). The theme topics consisted of the Technology, Collaboration, the Application and Overall Success of the learning interaction.

Collaboration and Multi-touch display technology:

1. Collaboration through Multi-touch technology:
   a. Did you find that the multi-touch display technology encourages discussion?
   b. Did you find that the multi-touch display technology encourages collaboration?
   c. Do you feel that the multi-touch display technology, which offers children to work in the same shared physical workspace, effectively facilitates collaborative learning?
2. Collaboration through Task Analysis and Breakdown
   a. Did you find that the breakdown of learning tasks encouraged discussion/collaboration

Fig 7: Sample Interview Themes.

The researchers acted as the facilitators to guide the group in a discussion to express their opinions and feelings. The sessions, situated in a meeting room at the Monash Faculty of IT, commenced with a 20 minute group interaction on the application on a large scale shared digital space. This was followed by a 40 minute focus group session to discuss four themes to ascertain the experts points of view (Vaughan, Schumm & Sinagub 1996). The sessions were recorded using an audiotape and then transcribed, summarised and analysed. During the sessions extensive notes were taken on observations of the participants nonverbal and verbal responses as these assisted in the interpretation of the findings (Vaughan, Schumm & Sinagub 1996).

Evaluation

Evaluation of the technology and the Phonics application was undertaken in two phases: the first being application use and survey by 19 general adult users (n = 19) to examine such aspects as Look and Feel, Usability, and Suitability of the Multi-touch Technology; and the second being application use and focus group sessions by 6 participants, who were university staff from the Faculty of Education, early-childhood experts and primary school teachers. Evaluation data from these two sources is presented together, under the contexts of Socio-Cultural theory and Distributed Cognition/Activity theory. Elements of this data have been reported in McGivern et. al. (2011) under the initial categorisation scheme, however it is important to consider other aspects of this data in relation to the educational theories and issues discussed above.

Socio-Cultural Theory:

As suggested previously, Socio-Cultural theory focuses on how people relate to each other in an interactive social context. A number of quantitative and qualitative survey questions were asked in the first phase of data collection relating to this issue. One question, in the context of usability, asked "Did you find you interacted verbally with your partner about the task at hand?". This question sought to determine the extent to which users communicated with each other during use of the application. All 19 participants replied positively.

The associated qualitative question provided insight into the nature of the verbal interactions taking place. 14 participants provided a response, with 9 indicating specific collaborative dialogue that took place throughout the activity. This included such teamwork as asking for letters ("I asked him for the correct letter"), helping each other in identifying letters and sounds ("He'd tell me when the letters were wrong & help me pick an appropriate one"), and general discussion regarding the task ("talking to each other about the letter required or the word in question"). It is important to note that at no point was the need for dialogue between participants made explicit. No part of the process or application requested that verbal interaction take place, suggesting that the design of the task and application promoted social interactions intuitively.

Two questions regarding the multi-touch technology also provide insight into the Socio-Cultural elements at work. Participants were asked if they found that the multi-touch technology encouraged collaboration and also discussion. Figure 8 below highlights the participant responses (on a 5-point Likert scale). As can be seen, participants very strongly felt that the technology encouraged discussion and especially collaboration. Given that collaboration could be of many different forms, it is unsurprising that this ranked slightly higher than discussion specifically, as collaborative interactions could also involve joint manipulation of objects on the shared workspace. A Chi-Square analysis of these responses showed a statistically significant response with regards to collaboration (p = 0.030), with responses clearly skewed toward a positive perception. While Chi-Square analysis regarding discussion did not prove statistically significant (p = 0.135), a very strong positive response was still shown given the small size of the participant pool. Participants were also invited to provide general comment on the multi-touch technology in this context. Several participants made specific mention of the collaborative nature of the technology, with one participant indicating that "It felt natural to help out your team mate" and another specifically suggesting that they felt "The collaboration helps users learn more effectively".

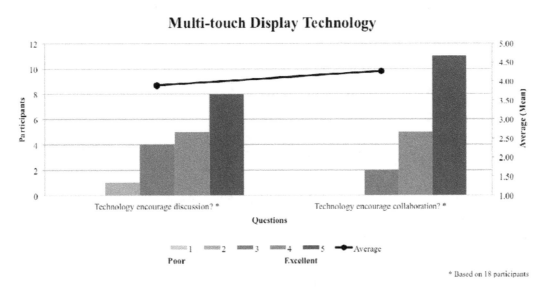

Fig 8: Participant Perception of Multi-touch Display Technology

These sentiments were also echoed by the focus group of early-childhood experts and teachers. During the course of the focus group, various comments emerged discussing the social nature of the interactions they believed would emerge once children were able use the technology and application. One participant in particular was quite excited at the social aspects:

> "I work with early childhood, usually, preschool. ...I think that is the most exciting things, in terms of technology for children as they can all gather around it, touching it, be doing it together..."

Another participant had the same expectation, especially when in comparison to other technologies such as data projectors and interactive whiteboards:

> "... whereas the screen when it is up on the wall, you can't get collaboration when it is up on the wall. It is like having a water table or your sand tray, but it is technology."

Focus group participants were also specifically asked to comment on the multi-touch technology and its role in encouraging discussion amongst users. One participant could envisage the large-scale nature of it leading directly to increased dialogue:

> "It does in the format that you showed me, because if you have got two children sitting on either side, they naturally have to talk to each other, because they can't complete this task essentially on their own... ...and, as what most people would do, is ask each other for help: Oh can you give me a letter A or D. ..and if children were doing this, and you were sounding out, for example 'dog' ...d...d...og. The kids could ask, 'Can you touch that again?' ...when facing each other they will communicate better..."

Distributed Cognition/Activity Theory:

As discussed earlier, Distributed Cognition/Activity theory examines how individuals interact in their environment, through the use of tools, resources and materials. The results of the study can be examined with a stronger focus on the design of the application and how it mediates interaction as opposed to the multi-touch technology in general.

Two significant questions were posed to the 19 participants of Phase One regarding the nature of the application, interactions with it, and how division of tasks within the application helped achieve the main goal. Participants were asked if they felt the structure of the application was goal oriented. Of the 19 participants 15 felt it was, while 4 disagreed. Of the 4 disagreements, all elaborated not that they felt the application was problematic, only that more hints or instructions were needed. For the vast majority however, the structure of the application and the division of tasks was clear. Following on from this, participants were also asked if the on-screen interactions were logical in achieving the tasks. In this case all 19 participants responded positively, suggesting again that the division of tasks amongst the pairs was an appropriate way to approach the learning task.

Focus group participants also provided insight into the success of a Distributed Cognition/Activity approach. Throughout the discussion, the design of the application and its ability to facilitate collaboration was positively highlighted. One participant noted that the application was designed such that it would be particularly engaging and would focus the children on the important aspects of the task:

> "It's bright, it's clear it's not too busy on the screen, the kids are able to focus exactly where they need to be, because kids easily get distracted in a busy...busy classroom..."

One participant provided insight into the arrangement of users around the large share digital space. Whereas participants were arranged on opposite sides, they saw great advantage to designing the application so that users were side-by-side:

> "I would use space to try shape the practice of the kids as to say that they are completely reliant on each other co-operation, one has to call out what they need and the other has to find it and give it, I like that but I am thinking that the side-by-side would work, but that is an interesting dimension there, you could have three people side-by-side. One person either side feeding in letters or images and letters or colours and shapes and the person in the middle can be the mediator, can be... construct the word, the image, the jig- saw, do you know what I mean?"

Several other participants became excited and engaged in a dialogue together on how the task distribution in the phonics study could be translated to other contexts:

> " What do you think about all the open ended 'stuff', potentially open ended ...not like this, that is structured? What do you think about the opportunities for open ended stuff?"

> "Look, I am not IT at all...I don't know how that would work, if it was a group activity that inspired conversation and a number of different solutions, yes, that's great. And, as you know from the Maths

point of view, there's two or three different ways of doing a maths problem, so, it therefore facilitates the different ways of learning that kids have...Yeah, I think that that would be good..."

Overall, the participants across both data collection phases considered the phonics application on the large shared digital space visually appealing and that it would encourage natural discussion and collaboration between children. They also believed that the large shared digital space was educational for children and that it was easy to use, innate, through direct manipulation. However, there is a need to improve several aspects of the design in order to increase the instructional effectiveness of the package before an evaluation involving children was commenced.

Conclusions and Further Research

This paper has detailed the theoretical foundations used to develop educational applications on large shared digital spaces in the form of Socio-Cultural theory and Distributed Cognition/Activity theory. A rationale has been provided to justify the technique of promoting learning by first engaging learners in a shared 'interpersonal' representation of a learning task, which can later be internalised. Also discussed is the need to engage peers in the shared learning activity through task division and role assignment in order to promote effective learning activity and to maximise communication between learners. A further theoretical perspective has been suggested by the use of Distributed Cognition/Activity theory to inform the design of large shared digital learning spaces in order to better understand the complexities of a cognitive system involving multiple people, activities and mediating artefacts. Also reported were the results from an evaluation of a Phonics application, with an emphasis on data relating to the theoretical perspectives discussed above. These results suggest that well designed learning interactions on large share digital spaces can indeed engender the types of collaborative activity and communications between learners required to promote Socio-Cultural learning effects. However careful consideration needs to be given to the distribution of tasks and roles, the arrangement of learners about the display, and the provision of well designed interface elements to support the activity of learners.

Further research will consist of evaluating a revised Phonics application with young learners in the classroom. A revised interface layout and interaction flow has been developed and is depicted in Figure 9.

Two Learner Application

1. Learner 2 selects a picture representing a word.
2. Learner 1 taps the picture to hear the word.
3. Learner 1 taps letters to hear them and requests missing letters.
4. Learner 2 taps letters to find the missing letter and passes it to Learner 1

Fig 9: The Revised Phonics Application Design

In this version of the application learners are grouped side by side in order to reduce difficulties associated with reading flipped letter tiles and words. Several interface and interaction issues will also be addressed in order to increase the ease of use of the Phonics application. Also under consideration is the extension of the principles and task division and role assignment to subject matter in the mathematics and physics domains.

Acknowledgements

The authors would like to express their appreciation of the generous support from the eEducation Centre, the Berwick Campus and the Faculty of Information Technology at Monash University, who funded this research.

References

Anderson, J. R. (2000). *Learning and memory: an integrated approach* (2 ed.). New York: John Wiley & Sons.

Brown, A. L. (1992). Design Experiments: Theoretical and Methodological Challenges in Creating Complex Interventions in Classroom Settings. *The Journal of the Learning Sciences, 2*(2), 141-178.

Butler, M. W., McGivern, D., Artmann, A. N., Morgan, M. (2010), *Multi-touch display technology and collaborative learning tasks*, Proceedings of the World Conference on Educational Multimedia, Hypermedia & Telecommunications (ED-MEDIA 2010), 29 June 2010 to 02 July 2010, Association for the Advancement of Computing in Education (AACE), Chesapeake VA USA, pp. 1441-1448.

Daniels, H. (2001). *Vygotsky and Pedagogy*. London: RoutledgeFalmer.

Daniels, H. (2005). The development of Vygotsky's thought An introduction to *Thinking and Speech*. In H. Daniels (Ed.), *An Introduction to Vygotsky*. New York: Routledge.

Dillenbourg, P., & Evans, M. (2011). Interactive tabletops in education. *International Journal of Computer-Supported Collaborative Learning*, 6(4), 491-514. doi: 10.1007/s11412-011-9127-7

Eggen, P., & Kauchak, D. (2007). *Educational Psychology: Windows on Classrooms* (7 ed.): Prentice Hall.

Engeström, Y. (2001). Expansive Learning at Work: Toward an activity theoretical reconceptualization. *Journal of Education and Work, 14*(1), 133-156. doi: 10.1080/13639080020028747

Fernyhough, C. (2008). Getting Vygotskian about theory of mind: Mediation, dialogue, and the development of social understanding. *Developmental Review, 28*(2), 225-262. doi: 10.1016/j.dr.2007.03.001

Fox, J. E., & Schirrmacher, R. (2011). *Art and Creative Development for Young Children*: Cengage Learning.

Hatano, G., & Inagaki, K. (1991). Sharing Cognition Through Collective Comprehension Activity. In L. B. Resnick, J. M. Levine & S. D. Teasley (Eds.), *Perspectives on Socially Shared Cognition* (pp. 331-348). Washington: American Psychological Association.

Higgins, S., Mercier, E., Burd, E., & Hatch, A. (2011). Multi-touch tables and the relationship with collaborative classroom pedagogies: A synthetic review. *International Journal of Computer-Supported Collaborative Learning*, 6(4), 515-538.

Hill, S. (2006). *Developing early literacy: assessment and teaching*. Prahran: Elenor Curtain Publishing.

Hollan, J., Hutchins, E., & Kirsh, D. (2000). Distributed cognition: toward a new foundation for human-computer interaction research. *ACM Trans. Comput.-Hum. Interact., 7*(2), 174-196. doi: 10.1145/353485.353487.

Hutchins, E. (1995). *Cognition in the Wild*: The MIT Press.

John-Steiner, V., & Mahn, H. (1996). Sociocultural approaches to learning and development: A Vygotskian framework. *Educational Psychologist, 31*(3-4), 191-206. doi: 10.1080/00461520.1996.9653266

Jonassen, D. H., & Reeves, T. C. (1996). Learning with technology: Using computers as cognitive tools. In D. H. Jonassen (Ed.), *Handbook of research for educational communications and technology* (pp. 693-719). New York: Simon & Schuster.

Khandelwal, M & Mazalek A 2007, 'Teaching table: a tangible mentor for pre-k math education', 15-17 February 2007, *Proceedings of the 1st international con- ference on Tangible and embedded interaction*, ACM, Baton Rouge, Louisiana, pp. 191-194.

Kumar, R 2005, *Research Methodology: A Step-by-Step Guide for Beginners*, Sage Publications, London.

McGivern, D., Butler, M. W., Morgan, M., 2011, *Using multi-touch display technology to support remedial phonics instruction techniques in collaborative learning environments*, Proceedings of Global Learn Asia Pacific 2011, 28 March 2011 to 01 April 2011, Association for the Advancement of Computing in Education, Chesapeake VA USA, pp. 56-64.

Morgan, M. & Butler, M. (2009) Considering Multi-touch Display Technology for Collaboration in the Classroom. In *Proceedings of World Conference on Educational Multimedia, Hypermedia and Telecommunications 2009* (pp. 674-683). Chesapeake, VA: AACE. Honolulu, HI, 21 June – 26 June.

Nardi, B., ed. (1996). *Context and Consciousness: Activity Theory and Human-Computer Interaction*, Cambridge: MIT Press.

Piper, AM & Hollan, JD 2009, 'Tabletop displays for small group study: affordances of paper and digital materials', *Proceedings of the 27th international conference on Human factors in computing systems*, 8 April 2009, ACM, Bos- ton, MA, USA, pp. 1227-1236.

Piper, A M, O'Brien, E, Morris, MR & Winograd T 2006, 'SIDES: a coopera- tive tabletop computer game for social skills development', *Proceedings of the 2006 20th anniversary conference on Computer supported cooperative work*, ACM, 4-8 November 2006, Banff, Alberta, Canada, pp. 1-10.

Roberts, J. (1964). The self-management of cultures. In W. Goodenough (Ed.), *Explorations in Cultural Anthropology: Essays in Honor of George Peter Murdock*: McGraw-Hill.

Sharp, H, Rogers, Y & Preece, J 2007, *Interaction Design: Beyond Human-Computer Interaction*, Wiley, West Sussex.

Terry, W. S. (2009). *Learning and memory: basic principles, processes, and procedures* (4th ed.). Boston: Pearson Education.

Turner, P., & McEwan, T. (2004). Activity Theory: Another Perspective on Task Analysis. In D. Diaper & N. Stanton (Eds.), *The handbook of task analysis for human-computer interaction* (pp. 423-440). Mahwah: Lawrence Erlbaum.

U.S. Department of Education Office of Elementary and Secondary_Education (2002). *Guidance for the Reading First Program.* Department of Education. Retrieved April 4, 2009 from http://www.ed.gov/programs/readingfirst/guidance.pdf

Vaughan, S, Schumm, JS & Sinagub, J 1996, *Focus group interviews in education and psychology*, SAGE Publications.

Vygotsky, L. S. (1997). The Problem of Consciousness. In R. W. Rieber & J. Wollock (Eds.), *The Collected works of L. S. Vygotsky* (Vol. 3, pp. 129-138). New York: Plenum Press.

Vygotsky, L. S. (1978). *Mind in Society: the development of higher psychological processes* (M. Cole, Trans.). Harvard Uni Press.

Wertsch, J. V. (1985). *Vygotsky and the social formation of mind*: Harvard University Press.

Wertsch, J. V., & Stone, C. A. (1986). The concept of internalization in Vygotsky's account of the genesis of higher mental functions. In J. V. Wertsch (Ed.), *Culture, communication, and cognition: Vygotskian perspectives*: Cambridge University Press.

Wood, D., Bruner, J. S., & Ross, G. (1976). The Role of Tutoring in Problem Solving*. *Journal of Child Psychology and Psychiatry, 17*(2), 89-100. doi: 10.1111/j.1469-7610.1976.tb00381.x

2 Assessing the Correlations Among Cognitive Overload, Online Course Design and Student Self-efficacy

Mohamed Ibrahim, Rebecca A. Callaway

Introduction

The majority of colleges and universities in the United States provide online courses, but the decision to offer courses online varies among the different types of institutions. Within the private four-year college community 60% of the institutions offer online courses as compared to 71% of for-profit colleges and universities. Public institutions indicate even more involvement with 89% of public four-year colleges and universities offering online courses. Two-year colleges show the highest interest with 91% of these institutions providing courses online (Parker, Lenhart & Moore, 2011).

Despite the overall growth of online learning in higher education, there are many issues facing students in this learning environment (e.g. course design complexity, navigation ease of the learning content, fluency in online terminologies, comfort and satisfaction issues, and self-efficacy) (DeTure, 2004; Preece, 2002; Swan, 2001). According to social cognitive theory, self-efficacy is the belief "in one's capabilities to organize and execute the courses of action required to produce given attainments" (Bandura, 1997). Self-efficacy becomes increasingly important for student success in an asynchronous online learning environment as the absence of instant access to the instructor prevents the student from receiving immediate formative feedback. Thus, the student must initially determine if their navigation, interpretation of instructions, comprehension of content and plan of action are correct. Difficulty comprehending content or initial confusion regarding online navigation or instructions can result in a lack of confidence and low self-efficacy. Individuals with low self-efficacy are less likely to perform related behaviors in the future. Consequently, a student with low self-efficacy may be less likely to attempt assignments perceived as similar to previous assignments in which they that were not successful. Thus, students with low self-efficacy may be less likely to succeed in an online course than those with higher levels of self-efficacy.

The design of learning materials is an essential component of student success in the online environment. Online courses that are designed based on cognitive science principles "assist students in managing their cognitive load and focusing their cognitive resources during learning and problem solving" (Chandler & Sweller, 1991). Learners are affected by the way the learning materials are designed and are more likely to gain deeper conceptual understanding from the content designed based on CTML (Baggett, 1984; Mayer, 2002; Mayer & Moreno, 2002). While multimedia design techniques have been investigated in relation to students' knowledge acquisitions in face-to-face and online, the present study examines the relationship between online course design and student self-efficacy. Students experiencing cognitive overload are predicted to display weak self-efficacy beliefs. Online courses based on CTML are expected to reduce students' cognitive load to perform the online tasks and produce students with higher levels of self-efficacy.

Theoretical Framework

Self-efficacy and Online Learning

According to social cognitive theory (Bandura, 1997) self-efficacy is a form of self-judgment that influences decisions about what behaviors to undertake, the amount of effort and persistence put forth when faced with obstacles, and finally, the mastery of the behavior. According to this theory, self-efficacy is not a measure of skill; rather, it reflects what individuals believe they can do with the skills they possess. For example, in discussing self-efficacy in computer use, Compeau and Higgins (1995) distinguished between component skills such as formatting disks and booting up the computer and behaviors individuals can accomplish with such skills, such as using software to analyze data. Thus, online self-efficacy focuses on what a person believes he or she can accomplish online. It does not refer to a person's skill at performing specific online learning related tasks (e.g. learning the materials, submitting assignments, or taking an online test). Instead, it assesses a person's judgment of his or her ability to apply knowledge and skills in a broader context, such as navigating the course content, finding and interpreting information or troubleshooting problems.

Participating in an online course is a complex task requiring skills and knowledge of computers and the online environment. Self-efficacy beliefs are a key component for novice students' success in overcoming the fear they may experience in the online environment. For example, Compeau and Higgins (1995) empirically verified the relationship between computer self-efficacy and computer use. Staples, Hulland, and Higgins (1999) found that those with high levels of self-efficacy in remote computing situations were more productive and satisfied, and better able to cope when working remotely. Consequently, students enrolled in an online course require development of a further set of skills. Online self-efficacy may be distinguished from computer self-efficacy as the belief that one can successfully perform a distinct set of behaviors required to establish, maintain and utilize effectively the online learning tasks beyond basic personal Internet and computer skills. These skills include navigating the course materials, familiarity with the online tools and terminologies, and locating relevant information.

Cognitive Theory of Multimedia Learning

Cognitive Theory of Multimedia Learning (CTML) design techniques reduce learners' cognitive loads and lessen the knowledge acquisition challenges associated with processing information from learning materials with multiple representations (visual and auditory). A number of prescriptive principles that guide the creation of learning materials align with human cognitive architecture. These design principles can be categorized into two groups: strategies to reduce extraneous cognitive load or strategies to increase germane load. Strategies to reduce extraneous cognitive load include signaling the main ideas and eliminating unnecessary content. Intrinsic cognitive load (i.e., essential processing related to the learning goal) is enhanced with various techniques such as segmentation. With segmentation, learning material is broken up into several segments of information to help students' process one cluster of related information elements before moving to the next one (Mayer, 1996).

The CTML design techniques are based on assumptions regarding the relationship between cognition and learning from dual representation information formats. Five of these assumptions are particularly relevant to learning from dual representation learning materials. First, the human mind consists of an unlimited, long-term memory in which prior knowledge is stored and a limited working memory where new information is processed. Second, that the working memory has two distinct channels for processing information; a visual/pictorial channel and an auditory/verbal channel. (Clark & Paivio, 1991). Third, each channel has limited capacity for information that can be processed at one time (Baddeley, 1986; Baddeley & Logie, 1999). Fourth, humans actively select relevant verbal and non-verbal information, organize the selected information into cognitive structures, and integrate these cognitive structures with the existing knowledge to construct a new (or update an old) mental representation (Mayer, 1996). Finally, humans are typically exposed to three types of cognitive load that compete for the limited resources of working memory: (1) intrinsic load, the cognitive processing required to comprehend content, (2) extraneous load, caused by ineffective formats of content presentation, and (3) germane load, which enables learners to engage in deeper cognitive processing of the material to be learned (Sweller, Van Merriënboer & Paas, 1998).

Research Questions

Three main questions are addressed in this study: 1) Is there a relationship between course design and students' cognitive overload, 2) Is there a relationship between students' perceived self-efficacy and cognitive overload and 3) Is there a relationship between students' perceived self-efficacy and course design?

This study examines how the segmentation of content in online learning environment affects students' cognitive load as compared to students learning from a non-segmentation version of the same content and provides a theoretical and empirical basis for the effect segmentation may have on students self-efficacy in the online learning environment. Unfortunately, many of the design techniques used in an online environment today reflect the subjective perceptions of —what works best acquired through the designer's personal experience and what designers considered best practices in the field, rather than empirical evidence (Najjar, 2001; Wetzel, et al., 1994).

According to CTML, when multimedia learning materials are designed using short concise segments, it helps reduce extraneous cognitive load (as reflected by perceived learning difficulty; Kalyuga, Chandler, & Sweller, 1999) because the learner is primed to engage in the processing of conceptually distinct clusters of information elements (Mautone & Mayer, 2001; Mayer, et al., 2002; Moreno & Mayer, 1999; Pollock, et al., 2002). In contrast, long instructional material consumes the learner's limited cognitive resources and results in increased extraneous cognitive load (Brünken, Plass, & Leutner, 2004; Cennamo, 1993).

Is there a relationship between course design and students' cognitive overload? Applying segmentation in an online module may decrease students' perceived learning difficulty. Moreno (2007) observed that participants who studied a segmented version of a classroom video or an animation reported lower mental effort and perceived the learning materials as less difficult than participants who studied using non-segmented versions of the same material. Similarly, participants self-reported a decrease in mental effort in a study using a segmented narrated animation as compared to those viewing a continuously narrated animation (Mayer & Chandler, 2001).

Is there a relationship between students' perceived self-efficacy and cognitive overload? Segmenting the online learning module may help students in their cognitive process through organizing and integrating the learning content, which may result in improving their self-efficacy. Cognitive science research suggests that novice learners do not seem to have enough time to engage in adequate processing of verbal and visual information when they are exposed to multimedia presentations (Mayer & Chandler, 2001). Thus, students who view segmented modules may have more cognitive resources to outperform students in the non-segmented conditions and consequently would have a better self-efficacy perception.

Is there a relationship between students' perceived self-efficacy and course design? Students learning from a segmented module may have more cognitive control over the short segments of the learning module, thus engaging in more meaningful learning and feeling more confident to complete the online learning tasks compared to students provided a non-segmented learning module. This hypothesis is supported by the results of a study in which students in a segmented video group outperformed the non-segmented group on retention tests (Moreno, 2007).

Method and Procedures

This study used a quasi-experimental research design between subjects to assess the relationship between the design aspects of an online course and students reported self-efficacy. The module design includes one of the CTML design techniques: segmentation (independent variable) and students reported self-efficacy and the perceived difficulty of the learning content as dependent variables.

Participants

Twenty-two junior and senior early childhood education majors participated in the study. Participants were enrolled in two BlackBoard sections of a required educational technology course. Course design, course material and evaluation were identical in both sections. Participation in the study was voluntary, with students opting in to the study receiving bonus points for their involvement.

Instrumentation

Perceived difficulty survey:

This questionnaire consisted of one Likert-scale self-report question to assess participants' perceived difficulty associated with learning from the online module. The questionnaire asks participants to indicate the degree of difficulty experienced from the learning content (from 1 = extremely easy, to 9 = extremely difficult). Participants reported the level of their perceived difficulty by placing a check mark next to one of the nine items that applied to them. This questionnaire was based on a survey developed by Paas & Merrienboer (1994) and updated by Kalyuga, Chandler, & Sweller (1999) and has been validated in other studies. Reliability of the scale with a population of college students was estimated with Cronbach's coefficient α at .90 (Paas & Van Merrienboer, 1994).

Self-efficacy survey:

This questionnaire was developed to assess the level of students' self-efficacy in online learning environment before and after completing the learning materials. The survey was based on a scale developed by

Bandura, A. (2001) and has been validated in other studies. Reliability of the scale with a population of college students was estimated with Cronbach coefficient α ranged 0.82 to 0.92 (Uzuntiryaki & Çapa, 2009).

Materials

The instructional materials were online modules in an educational technology course designed for elementary education majors. A chapter from an instructional technology textbook on integrating technology into the language arts classroom served as the basis for the modules. The online modules were identical in instructional material content, yet differed in organization (i.e. segmented and non-segmented). The non-segmented module consisted of the complete chapter online with no change in organization or layout. The segmented module consisted of the material from the 20-page chapter chunked into six coherent learning segments. Although the segmented and non-segmented learning materials were identical in content, the length of each segment in the segmented condition was relatively short (3-4 pages). The non-segmented group read the 20 pages and answered a series of questions and reflected on their reading at the conclusion of the module. The segmented group was exposed to a series of modules, answering questions and reflecting on their reading after each module.

Procedure

The two groups learned from two different designs: students randomly assigned to one group received the non-segmented module, while the other group received the segmented module treatment. Both modules were identical in length and content and were designed by the same instructional designer. Students in both groups completed a self-efficacy survey prior to beginning the learning module. After completing the online modules (segmented and the non-segmented) students completed the perceived difficulty survey and the self-efficacy survey a second time.

Results

Is there a relationship between course design and students' cognitive overload?

After checking the normality of the dependent variable distribution, a one-sample t-test revealed a statistically reliable difference between the mean number of students reported perceived difficulty of the learning materials in the online segmented module (M = 11.1, SD = 10.6), $t(8) = 0.01$), $p < .05$, compared to students in the non-segmented module (M = 11.1, SD = 15.7), $t(8) = 0.07$).

Table 1 shows the t-test result, including mean scores and standard deviations for the segmented and non-segmented groups on the measures of difficulty rating.

Table 1

Mean scores and standard deviations for the segmented and non-segmented groups on the measures of difficulty rating

	t	df	Sig. (2-tailed)	Mean Difference
Course design	13.748	21	.000	1.5
Cognitive Load in segmented	3.162	8	.013	11.1
Cognitive Load in non-segmented	2.121	8	.067	11.1

Note. Means with different subscripts differ significantly at p<.05

Is there relationship between students' perceived self-efficacy and cognitive overload?

A partial correlation analysis was conducted after controlling for the effect of the prior self-efficacy rating. The results indicated that the perceived difficulty of the learning materials reported by students in the segmented module condition does not correlate with their perceived self-efficacy. However, the perceived difficulty of the learning module reported by students in the non-segmented module positively correlated with their perceived self-efficacy, Pearson's $r(4) = .80, p < .05$. Table 2 summarizes the analysis.

Table 2
Partial correlation Coefficient (controlling for effect of the self-efficacy rating before taking the modules) for relationship between students' perceived self-efficacy and cognitive overload variables

		Self-efficacy Questions		
		Question1	Question 2	Question 3
Segmented	Correlation	.151	.151	.151
	Significance (1-tailed)	.387	.387	.387
Non-segmented	Correlation	.801*	.801*	.801*
	Significance (1-tailed)	.028	.028	.028

Note.   1.   Means   with   different   subscripts   differ   significantly   at   p<.05.
2. (.) Correlation is significant at the 0.05 level*

Is there a relationship between students' perceived self-efficacy and course design?

A Pearson product-moment correlation coefficient was conducted resulting in a positive correlation between the two variables in the modified and the non-modified condition. Results for the segmented module condition were: $r = 0.569, n = 11, p < 0.05$; the non-segmented module condition produced $r = 0.535, n = 11, p < 0.05$. Overall, there was a strong, positive correlation between students' perceived self-efficacy and course design. Table 3 and 4 summarize the results.

Table 3
Correlation Coefficient for relationship between students' perceived self-efficacy and course design

	Segmented module	Before
Segmented module	Pearson Correlation	.569*⃰
	Sig. (1-tailed)	.034
	Non-segmented module	**Before**
Non-segmented module	Pearson Correlation	.535*
	Sig. (1-tailed)	.045

*Note. *. Correlation is significant at the 0.05 level (1-tailed).*

General Discussion

Self-efficacy is very important variable in completion of any learning task, whether learning takes place online or face-to-face. This study was interested in investigating students' self-efficacy in relationship to the online course design only. Investigators employed a CTML design principle (segmentation) to reduce novice learners' extraneous cognitive load and its effect on students' self-efficacy perception.

Findings of this study revealed that there was a statistically significant difference between the perceived difficulties of the learning materials reported by students in the segmented module compared to students in the non-segmented module. This result supports CTML's underlying assumption that working memory has a limited capacity, and the human mind can only process small portions of large amounts of learning content at one time. The results also support previous findings produced in the context of learning from educational animations and video and provide empirical evidence that validates this theory. Furthermore, findings are consistent with the evidence that segmenting the learning content reduces students' perceived cognitive load by breaking down the learning material into small units (Mautone & Mayer, 2001; Mayer & Moreno, 2003).

A possible interpretation of this result is that the segmentation principle used in the present study helped reduce students' perception of the learning difficulty by chunking 20 pages of a textbook into six coherent learning segments. Although the segmented and non-segmented learning materials have identical content, the length of each segment in the segmented condition was relatively short (3-4 pages). Consequently, segmenting the content contributed to the optimization of learners' knowledge integration processes during studying (Mayer & Moreno, 2003). In the non-segmented condition however, learners were not able to process information as effectively and efficiently because the length of novel information without explicit breaks interfered with the organization and integration of individual information segments.

The results indicated that the perceived difficulty of the learning materials reported by students in the segmented module does not correlate with their perceived self-efficacy while the perceived difficulty of the learning module reported by students in the non-segmented module positively correlated with their perceived self-efficacy. While this result suggests that the segmentation principle does not improve students' self-efficacy perception in the online learning environment there must be other variable responsible for this difference such as in the population or the course design. A possible interpretation for this result is that students in both groups have similar level of confidence to complete their learning task in online learning environment. This confidence includes their judgment of their ability to apply knowledge and skills in a broader context, finding and interpreting information or troubleshooting problems in the learning content. Moreover, both groups in this study are familiar with online learning environment and were able to complete successfully other online courses and perform the distinct set of behaviors required to establish, maintain and utilize effectively the online learning tasks beyond basic personal Internet and computer skills. These skills include navigating the course materials, familiarity with the online tools and terminologies, and locating relevant information. This interpretation was confirmed through our third finding.

Finally, the results of this study indicate that although there was a strong and positive correlation between students' perceived self-efficacy and course design in both conditions, students in the segmented condition reported higher level of self-efficacy compared to students in the non-segmented group. A possible interpretation for this result is that although students in both groups have control over the learning content and both groups were able to navigate the learning materials on the same level, segmenting the 20 pages into small sections helped students in the segmented condition to feel more confident to complete the learning task. This result highlights the importance of taking into account the limitations of learners' working memory capacity in online learning environment, especially when learners have not developed domain-specific schemas that help them interpret this information (Kalyuga, Ayres, Chandler, & Sweller, 2003; Moreno & Duran, 2004). Unlike processing print text, which allows learner to read in a linear fashion, the online content design can affect students' navigation ability. Thus, more cognitive support, like segmenting is required for designing online learning modules.

Limitations

There are possible limitations related to the sampling and measurement used in this study. First, a convenience sample as employed to focus on one specific student population (i.e., novice, undergraduate, non-science majors enrolled in an education course), one particular domain (i.e., education), and a specific presentation format (i.e., online module). Furthermore, the fact that the content used in this study was relatively low in difficulty (i.e., integration of technology in English and Language Arts Instruction), suggests that it is possible that researchers working with more complex, and ill-structured topics and with other populations will produce entirely different results. For example, it has been consistently shown that cognitive support mechanisms are particularly effective when used with novice learners and complex topics (e.g., Shapiro, 2004). While the investigators attempted to control for as many differences between groups as possible, a quasi-experiment always runs the risk that prior differences exist between the groups on variables not measured, and these differences may cause differences in the outcome variables. However, we had no reason to suspect that the two groups of students enrolled in the same course in two intact sections would differ, as all students were non-science majors and generally in their junior or senior year of college.

Finally, using a self-report to measure learning difficulty and infer cognitive load is considered a limitation because this measure focuses narrowly on the content difficulty and does not include other critical aspects of cognitive load, such as mental effort and response time. However, finding a single valid measure of cognitive load continues to be a challenge for educational psychologists (e.g., DeLeeuw & Mayer, 2008).

References

Baddeley. (1986). *Working memory*. Oxford; New York: Clarendon Press ; Oxford University Press.

Baddeley, & Logie. (1999). Working memory: The multiple-component model. In A. Miyake & P. Shah (Eds.), *Models of working memory: mechanisms of active maintenance and executive control*. New York: Cambridge University Press.

Baggett, P. (1984). Role of temporal overlap of visual and auditory material in forming dual media associations. *Journal of Educational Psychology, 76*(3), 408-417.

Bandura, A. (1997). *Self-efficacy : the exercise of control*. New York: W.H. Freeman.

Bandura, A. (2001). *Guide for constructing self-efficacy scales*. Available from Albert Bandura, Department of Psychology, Stanford University, Standford, CA 94305-2130.

Brünken, R., Plass, L., & Leutner, D. (2004). Assessment of cognitive load in multimedia learning with dual-task methodology: Auditory load and modality effects. *Instructional Science, 32*(1-2), 1-2.

Chandler, & Sweller. (1991). Cognitive load theory and the format of instruction. *Cognition and Instruction, 8*(4), 293 - 332.

Clark, & Paivio. (1991). Dual coding theory and education. *Educational Psychology Review, 3*(3), 60.

Compeau, D. R., & Higgins, C. A. (1995). Computer Self-Efficacy: Development of a Measure and Initial Test. *MIS Quarterly, 19*(2), 189-211.

DeTure, M. (2004). Cognitive Style and Self-Efficacy: Predicting Student Success in Online Distance Education. *The American Journal of Distance Education, 18*(1), 21-38.

Kalyuga, S., Chandler, P., & Sweller, J. (1999). Managing split-attention and redundancy in multimedia instruction. *Applied Cognitive Psychology., 13*(4), 351.

Mautone, P., & Mayer, R. (2001). Signaling as a cognitive guide in multimedia learning. *Journal of Educational Psychology., 93*(2), 377.

Mayer. (1996). Learning Strategies for Making Sense out of Expository Text: The SOI Model for Guiding Three Cognitive Processes in Knowledge Construction. *Educational psychology review., 8*(4), 357.

Mayer. (2001). *Multimedia learning*. Cambridge; New York: Cambridge University Press.

Mayer. (2002). *The promise of educational psychology : Learning in the content areas*. Upper Saddle River, N.J.: Merrill.

Mayer, R. (2003). The promise of multimedia learning: Using the same instructional design methods across different media. *Learning and Instruction 13*(2), 125.

Mayer, R., & Chandler, P. (2001). When learning is just a click away: Does simple user interaction foster deeper understanding of multimedia messages? *Journal of Educational Psychology., 93*(2), 390.

Mayer, & Moreno. (2002). Animation as an aid to multimedia learning. *Educational Psychology Review, 14*, 87-100.

Moreno, R. (2007). Optimising learning from animations by minimising cognitive load: Cognitive and affective consequences of signalling and segmentation methods. *Applied Cgnitive Psychology, 21*(6), 765-781.

Najjar, L. (1996). Multimedia Information and Learning. *Journal of Educational Multimedia and Hypermedia, 5*(2), 129-150.

Paas, F., & Van Merrienboer, J. (1994). Instructional control of cognitive load in the training of complex cognitive tasks. *Educational Psychology Review, 6*(4), 351.

Parker, K., Lenhart, A., & Moore, K. (2011). The Digital Revolution and Higher Education: College Presidents, Public Differ on Value of Online Learning (Research). Retrieved October, 2011, from Pew Social & Demographic Trends

Pollock, E., Chandler, P., & Sweller, J. (2002). Assimilating complex information. *Learning and Instruction, 12*(1), 61-86.

Preece, J. (2002). Sociability and usability in online communities: determining and measuring success. *Communication Abstracts, 25*(4), 431-586.

Staples, D. S., Hulland, J. S., & Higgins, C. A. (1999). A Self-Efficacy Theory Explanation for the Management of Remote Workers in Virtual Organizations. *Organization Science, 10*(6), 758-776.

Swan, K. (2001). Virtual Interaction: Design Factors Affecting Student Satisfaction and Perceived Learning in Asynchronous Online Courses. *Distance Education, 22*(2), 306-331.

Sweller, J., Van Merriënboer, J., & Paas, F. (1998). Cognitive Architecture and Instructional Design. *Educational Psychology Review, 10*(3), 251-296.

Wetzel, C., Radtke, P., & Stern, H. (1994). *Instructional effectiveness of video media*: Lawrence Erlbaum Associates.

Uzuntiryaki, E., & Çapa, A. (2009). Development and Validation of Chemistry Self-Efficacy Scale for College Students. *Research in Science Education, 39,* 4, 539-551.

3 The Effects of Modality And Multimedia Comprehension on the Performance of Students with Varied Multimedia Comprehension Abilties When Exposed To High Complexity, Self-Paced Multimedia Instructional Materials

Daniah Al-Abbasi

INTRODUCTION

Utilizing multimedia in learning has become one of the revolutionary additions to education during the last few decades. Researchers were interested in finding and applying effective design principles in order to get the most benefit from the powerful capabilities of multimedia. However, empirically tested design principles are governed by specific conditions that are not applicable to all learning situations and learner abilities. Moreno (2006) suggested that more research is needed to fully understand the conditions governing the effective utilization of the modality effect in instruction. She further recommended studying the effects of individual differences especially in a high cognitive load environment that may affect learning from different modalities.

Low comprehenders suffer from a decreased ability for comprehending complex textual and pictorial materials (Maki & Maki, 2002). This deficit will lead to overloading their working memory, and consequently cause a decrease in their performance (Carretti et al., 2009). Similarly, Shute & Gawlick-Grendell (1994) compared high and low cognitive ability learners on the basis of learning from a computerized version of tutorial versus learning from a paper and pencil one. They found that low cognitive ability participants benefited less from learning from a computerized version of a workbook compared with learning from a paper and pencil version. They hypothesized that low-ability participants didn't benefit from the computerized version because it demanded more cognitive resources than what they could handle.

Based on the discussed findings of the previous research studies, the performance of individuals with multimedia comprehension difficulties may be improved if presented with a multimedia environment that is bimodal, self-paced, and follows effective design guidelines such as contiguity. So, the goal behind this research study was to explore multimedia comprehension as a factor that may affect students' learning performance when using of complex multimedia instructional materials and how modality of presentation mediates this effect.

The STUDY

The purpose of this research was to study the effects of modality and multimedia comprehension on the performance of students with varied multimedia comprehension abilities when exposed to high complexity, self-paced multimedia instructional materials.

For this study, participants' multimedia comprehension ability was measured with a standardized multimedia comprehension test called the multimedia comprehension battery (MMCB) to acquire a baseline score of their pretreatment multimedia comprehension level. Then, based on that level, participants were randomly assigned to two versions of the instructional materials. The first version was the bimodal, and the second version was the unimodal. Both versions had identical complexity instructional materials and both allowed for learner-paced control. Before exposure to the treatment conditions, students' prior knowledge on the tested subject was measured with a pretest. After exposure, posttests were administered to measure students' retention and transfer.

This study has employed a 2 x 2 generalized randomized block design with two levels of multimedia comprehension and two levels of modality. The two levels of multimedia comprehension were: below average and average and above. The two levels of modality were: bimodal (moving or still picture/narration) and unimodal (moving or still picture/text). The dependent variables were retention and transfer. Multivariate analysis of covariance (MANCOVA) was performed to test for possible interaction or main effects that may appear between the treatment groups. The covariates used are study time and pretest scores. The analysis was done using the latest version of SPSS® with alpha level of .05.

Materials

Multimedia Comprehension Battery (MMCB)

The MMCB (Gernsbacher & Varner, 1988) is an instrument developed to measure multimedia comprehension of three modality formats; visual, auditory, and pictorial. It is composed of six stimulus stories. Two are presented by written sentences, two are presented by spoken sentences, and two are presented by nonverbal pictures. The visual stories contain 636 and 585 words presented line by line at a rate of 185 words/min. The auditory stories contain 958 and 901 words read at a rate of 215 words/min. The pictorial stories contain 31 and 32 pictures affixed to projector slides with no words and presented at a rate of 7.75 seconds/slide. Each story is followed by 12 open ended comprehension questions. The instrument is designed to allow 20 seconds for answering each question. Moreover, the instrument gives an overall score of multimedia comprehension as well as a separate score of each modality format.

Later, Gernsbacher (1991) updated the instrument by creating a multiple-choice version of the comprehension questions of the visual and auditory stories. Austin and Maki (2002) converted the MMCB to an electronic format and created a multiple-choice version of the comprehension questions of the pictorial stories. In this study, Austin and Maki's version (2002) of the MMCB was used because it has been converted to an electronic format that can be incorporated easily into the study the materials, and it also had the multiple-choice version of the pictorial stories comprehension questions.

Treatment Conditions

Two treatment conditions were created from the designed program. The fixed design specifications that were shared between both conditions deal with complexity of the instructional materials, pacing of presentation, and effective screen design features such as contiguity. The only difference between the treatments was the modality of presentation.

Complexity. Regarding complexity, the subject of the instructional materials was life science and the topic was meiosis. The topic was chosen by a content expert who was asked to choose a topic high in its element interactivity based on his/her previous teaching experience. Choosing this type of content was imperative because unlike low element interactivity content, high element interactivity content places more load on the working memory (Sweller, Merrienboer, & Paas, 1998). This load negatively affects the performance of students low in multimedia comprehension skills more than students high in multimedia comprehension skills (Maki & Maki, 2002). Moreover, based on previous research results the modality effect mostly appears when participants are exposed to complex materials because it relieves some of the load imposed on the working memory (Ginns, 2005). So, by increasing and unifying the complexity of the materials in both treatment conditions we may be able to measure the true effects of modality on the performance of students with varying multimedia comprehension skills.

Pacing. The type of pacing chosen for presenting the instructional materials of both treatment conditions was self-pacing. Self-pacing was chosen to extract the variance associated with the effect of pacing from the treatments in order to measure the true effect of modality on participants' performance. This is because participants with reduced multimedia comprehension ability need more time to comprehend the materials compared with participants high in their multimedia comprehension ability. So, by giving both participant types flexible comprehension time, the variance associate with this individual difference may be eliminated, and therefore both types should have an equal chance to fully comprehend the materials.

Design. The screen design feature taken into account when designing the treatment conditions was contiguity. This is because contiguity has empirically demonstrated to affect students' performance in prior research (Austin, 2009). Austin found that repositioning text to be next to the animation rather than below it removed the modality effect that existed between the animation/narration condition and the animation/text condition. This means that repositioning the text relieved some of the load imposed on the working memory which made the modality effect disappears.

The reason of adding this screen design feature in this study was to eliminate the effect of improper screen design features that may affect students' performance beyond the effect of the treatment (modality). This is because the main goal behind this research was to understand the effect of multimedia comprehension ability on students' performance and whether this effect can be manipulated by changing the modality of presentation. Therefore, controlling for screen design may give us more accurate results because it may remove the variance associated with screen design. In the unimodal (moving or still picture/text) condition, text appeared as static block. In the bimodal

38

(moving or still picture/narration) condition, no text was added to the screen because text was narrated. A diagram of the screen showing the placement of the textual and pictorial elements is shown in figure 1.

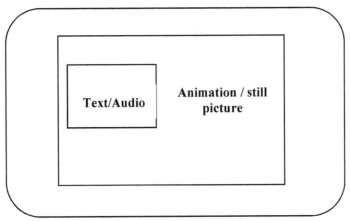

Figure 1. Screen design

Modality. The modality of presentation varied between the two conditions. In the first condition, both the visual and the auditory channels were utilized during the cognitive process. Therefore, dual modality was used by presenting the textual materials of the content in auditory format rather than visual format. So, the learner in this condition was able to listen to the textual materials and observe the pictorial materials. The pictorial content was presented as an animation and still pictures to ease intelligibility of the described process. In the second condition only the visual channel was utilized. Therefore, single modality was used by presenting the textual materials in a visual format rather than an auditory format. So, the learner had to read the textual materials and at the same time observe the pictorial materials. The pictorial materials were also presented as an animation and still pictures. The percentage of animated pictures in the instructional materials was approximately 30% while the percentage of still picture was approximately 70%. Screen shots of both conditions are presented in figures 2 & 3.

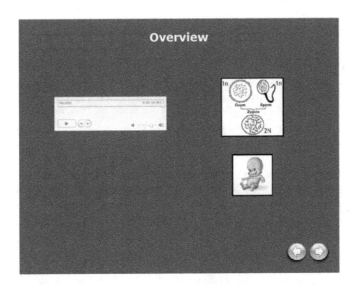

Figure 2. Bimodal condition

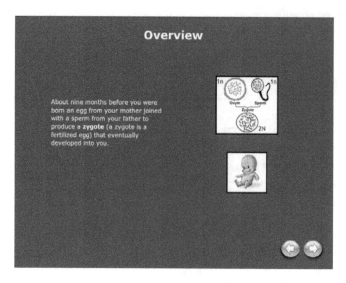

Figure 3. Unimodal condition

Study Time

Study time is the time spent by students in studying the multimedia lesson. Data collected from this variable were used as a covariate during data analysis to control for the variance associated with the time differences between students.

Pretest

The pretest was designed to contain 5 multiple-choice questions that measured participants' prior knowledge of the presented instructional materials. This measure was important because it helped us to control for experienced participants so their scores won't affect the results. To do this, pretest scores were used as a covariate during data analysis.

Posttests

The two designed posttest quizzes measured participants' retention and transfer ability of the taught instructional materials. The retention quiz was composed of 20 multiple-choice questions and the transfer test was composed of 10 multiple-choice questions. Students were allowed to answer the questions at their own pace. Each question had four multiple-choice answers. One of the answers was scored correct and the others were scored incorrect. Each correct answer in the retention quiz was given one point, giving an overall total of 20 points. Moreover, each correct answer in the transfer quiz was given 2 points, giving an overall total of 20 points. Participants' performance on the two quizzes helped find out whether there is a main, interaction effect, or both.

Retention test. The retention test measured participants' ability to remember the learned instructional materials as a result of being exposed to the treatment conditions. It gave us an indication of how well the treatment was successful in reaching the first stage of knowledge acquisition that is recall. To ensure validity and reliability, the questions of the retention test was created by a content expert to ensure their validity. Moreover, internal consistency of the questions was performed using Cronbach's alpha. The Cronbach's alpha value was found to be .68.

Transfer test. The transfer test measured participants' ability to apply the newly acquired knowledge to novel situations. It gave us more insight on how well the newly acquired knowledge has been deeply and meaningfully processed and comprehended. This level of comprehension is believed to be one of the highest levels of understanding. Also, as the case with the retention test, validity and reliability of the transfer test was ensured by asking a content expert to create the questions. Moreover, internal consistency of the questions was performed using Cronbach's alpha and its value was found to be .31.

40

RESEARCH QUESTIONS

1. What are the effects of modality (bimodal vs. unimodal) on the retention and transfer performance of college students studying a multimedia instructional presentation?
2. What are the effects of multimedia comprehension level (below average vs. average and above) on the retention and transfer performance of college students studying a multimedia instructional presentation?
3. How will modality and comprehension level interact to affect the retention and transfer performance of college students studying a multimedia instructional presentation?

MANCOVA RESULTS

A 2 x 2 two-way multivariate analysis of covariance (MANCOVA) [between-subjects factors: multimedia comprehension level (below average, average & above) and modality (bimodal, unimodal); covariates (pretest scores, study time)] revealed a non-significant main effect of modality on the dependent measures, Wilks's $\Lambda = .95$, $F(2,108) = 2.60$, $p > .05$. The multivariate partial η^2 based on Wilks's Λ was .05. So, the results showed no significant main effect of modality on students' performance in the retention and transfer tests.

The results also revealed a significant main effect of multimedia comprehension on the dependent measures, Wilks's $\Lambda = .89$, $F(2,108) = 6.64$, $p < .01$. The multivariate partial η^2 based on Wilks's Λ was .11. So, unlike modality, the results indicate a significant main effect of multimedia comprehension on students' performance in the retention and transfer tests.

Moreover, the results revealed a significant interaction effect of the multimedia comprehension factor and the modality factor on the dependent measures, Wilks's $\Lambda = .92$, $F(2,108) = 4.75$, $p < .05$. The multivariate partial η^2 based on Wilks's Λ was .08. So, modality coupled with multimedia comprehension was found to significantly affect students' performance in the retention and transfer tests. Table 4.6 summarizes the MANCOVA findings.

ANOVA RESULTS

Separate analyses of variances (ANOVA) for each dependent variable were conducted as follow-up tests to the MANCOVA. The ANOVA on retention for the modality factor was not significant, $F(1, 109) = 1.96$, $p > .05$, partial $\eta^2 = .02$, while the ANOVA on transfer for the same factor was significant, $F(1, 109) = 4.65$, $p < .05$, partial $\eta^2 = .04$. This indicates that for the modality factor, students' performance on the retention test did not vary significantly. However, modality had some effect on students' performance on the transfer test meaning that for the modality factor, students' performance on the transfer test did vary significantly.

The ANOVAs on retention, $F(1, 109) = 9.47$, $p < .01$, partial $\eta^2 = .08$, and transfer, $F(1, 109) = 7.99$, $p < .01$, partial $\eta^2 = .07$ for the multimedia comprehension factor were both significant. In other words, the multimedia comprehension factor significantly affected students' performance in the retention and transfer tests. Specifically, students in the average and above groups outperformed students in the below average groups in the retention and transfer tests.

Finally, the ANOVA on retention for the interaction effect was not significant $F(1, 109) = .86$, $p > .05$, partial $\eta^2 = .01$, while the ANOVA on transfer for the interaction effect was significant $F(1, 109) = 6.41$, $p < .05$, partial $\eta^2 = .06$. So, the results demonstrated a significant interaction effect of the transfer measure and not the retention measure. In fact, the results showed a significant interaction effect of modality and multimedia comprehension on the performance of the average and above students in the transfer test. Table 4.6 summarizes the MANCOVA and ANOVA findings.

Table 4.6

Multivariate and Univariate Analysis of Variance F Ratios for the Multimedia Comprehension X Modality on the Retention and Transfer Tests

| | | ANOVA | |
| | MANCOVA | Retention Measure | Transfer Measure |
Variable	$F(2,108)$	$F(1,109)$	$F(1,109)$
Modality (M)	2.60	1.96	4.65*
Multimedia Comprehension (MC)	6.64**	9.47**	7.99**
M X MC	4.75*	.86	6.41*

Note. F ratios are Wilks's approximation of Fs. MANCOVA = multivariate analysis of variance; ANOVA = univariate analysis of variance.

$*p < .05. **p < .01.$

DISCUSSIONS And CONCLUSION

The results of this study have demonstrated a significant main effect of multimedia comprehension on the retention and transfer performance of students. The performance of the average and above groups was significantly higher than the performance of the below average groups. This result has been demonstrated in past research and was attributed to individual differences. Gyselinck, et al. (2008) and others found that the difference in performance between the high-ability learners and the low-ability learners is related to difficulties in processing visual and verbal information that low-ability learners experience. This weakness prevents low-ability learners from constructing integrated mental representations of the selected visual and verbal information, which is imperative to meaningful learning. On the other hand, Gernsbacher and faust (1991) attributed the difference in performance to the lack of suppression that low-ability learners experience. They claim that during comprehension low-ability learners lose access to recently comprehended information much quicker than high-ability learners. Due to this problem, low-ability learners tend to shift more often and develop many substructures, which consequently lead to overloaded working memory and decreased performance.

The results have also demonstrated different effects of modality and multimedia comprehension on performance. Modality and multimedia comprehension had a non-significant effect on the retention and transfer performance of the below average students. Similarly, modality and multimedia comprehension had a non-significant effect on the retention performance of the average and above learners; however, modality and multimedia comprehension had a significant reversed effect on the transfer performance of those students. These different effects of modality and multimedia comprehension maybe related to several factors; pacing, multimedia comprehension ability, and type of posttest given.

The non-significant effect found in the transfer and retention performance of the below average learners maybe largely related to individual differences. Learners with reduced multimedia comprehension ability lack the suppression mechanism needed for effective comprehension (Gernsbacher & Faust, 1991). Therefore, in this study it has been found that using a unimodal or bimodal presentation didn't make a difference in performance, and so modality may not be the ideal solution to increase meaningful learning and improved performance. Another possible reason for the disappearance of the modality effect may be related to pacing. When self-pacing is allowed, learners can employ effective text processing strategies, which lower the load caused by the unimodal presentation on working memory, and therefore improve performance.

On the other hand, the non-significant effect found in the retention performance of the average and above learners and the significant reversed modality effect found in their transfer performance may not only be related to individual differences, but it may also be related to pacing, the complexity of the instructional materials, and the cognitive load related to the retention and transfer measures. When the complexity of the instructional materials is high and pacing is controlled by the learner, average and above learners in the unimodal condition utilize effective text processing strategies to fully and meaningfully comprehend the content (Cheon, Crooks, Inan, Flores, & Ari,

2011). According to the control of processing principle, utilizing such strategies makes the use of the unimodal presentation superior to the bimodal presentation (Schnotz, 2005). Moreover, the cognitive load associated with the retention measure is different than the one related to the transfer measure. The retention measure requires a storage only process, however the transfer measure requires storage and deep cognitive processing (Carretti et al., 2009). So, the load imposed on working memory because of the transfer task is higher than the one imposed by the retention measure.

This may explain why the modality effect disappeared in the retention performance and reversed in the transfer performance. In the retention performance, the modality effect disappeared because average and above learners in the unimodal presentation were able to utilize effective text processing strategies, which made their performance comparable to the bimodal group. Moreover, the low cognitive load imposed on working memory by the retention measure further contributes to this comparable performance result. However, in the transfer performance, average and above learners utilized effective text processing strategies, but this time, the transfer measure imposed a higher load on working memory which puts the unimodal presentation at a superior state over the bimodal presentation because of text processing strategies. This may have lead to a reversed modality effect.

IMPLICATIONS For INSTRUCTIONAL DESIGN

The results have shed some light on two major areas; the effect of multimedia comprehension ability on retention and transfer performance, and the effect of modality on retention and transfer performance of students with varied multimedia comprehension abilities.

As we have seen in the results of past research and the results of this research, individual differences have a significant effect on learners' performance. In this study, multimedia comprehension ability has demonstrated a significant effect on performance. Students high in multimedia comprehension ability outperformed students low in multimedia comprehension ability. Due to this important finding, multimedia comprehension ability should be taken into consideration when designing multimedia instructional materials.

As indicated in the results of this study, modality didn't exert any negative or positive effect on the retention and transfer performance of the below average learners. This means that modality may not be an important instructional design feature to improve the performance of below average learners. Therefore, other instructional design features should be considered. For example, incorporating advance organizers and/or review questions to promote deep thinking and meaningful learning.

Moreover, an important consideration to keep in mind when designing complex self-paced instructional materials for average and above learners is to use a unimodal presentation to allow students to utilize effective text processing strategies. This may contribute to an increase in performance especially if the teacher is considering assessing higher order thinking skills, such as administering a transfer test. On the other hand, if the teacher is not interested in assessing higher order thinking skills and is only interested in lower level skills such as retention, using a unimodal or bimodal presentation may not make a difference in the retention performance, and therefore both modality formats are feasible.

RECOMMENDATIONS For FUTURE RESEARCH

This study explored the effect of multimedia comprehension as an individual difference factor and found that it had a significant effect on performance. Students with below average multimedia comprehension ability performed significantly less than students with average and above multimedia comprehension ability.

Nowadays multimedia learning is becoming increasingly popular especially with the invention of mobile learning devices. Many schools are considering downloading and using e-books on personal tablets instead of using printed ones. E-books are loaded with multimedia and because of differences in multimedia comprehension ability we are going to have many disadvantaged learners. Therefore, extensive research should be conducted to further understand the effects of individual differences on performance (Gyselinck et al., 2008).

The second factor explored in this study was modality. The reason modality was chosen is to find out if modality can alleviate the load imposed on working memory and improve the performance of below average students. The results showed that modality had little or no effect on the performance of below average learners. Due to this result, future research should concentrate on finding effective instructional strategies that increase meaningful learning in a multimedia environment. An example for this is exploring the use of recall, organizational, integration, and elaboration strategies to overcome multimedia comprehension difficulties.

REFRENCES

Austin, K. (2009). Multimedia learning: Cognitive individual differences and display design techniques predict transfer learning with multimedia learning modules. *Computers & Education, 53*(4), 1339-1354.

Austin, K., & Maki, W. (2002). *Automated assessment of multimedia comprehension skills.* Texas Tech University. Lubbock, Texas.

Carretti, B., Borella, E., Cornoldi, C., & De Beni, R. (2009). Role of working memory in explaining the performance of individuals with specific reading comprehension difficulties: A meta-analysis. *Learning and Individual Differences, 19*(2), 246-251.

Cheon, J., Crooks, S., Inan, F., Flores, R., & Ari, F. (2011). Exploring the instructional conditions for a reverse modality effect in multimedia instruction. *Journal of Educational Multimedia and Hypermedia, 20*(2), 117-133.

Gernsbacher, M. A., & Faust, M. E. (1991). The mechanism of suppression: A component of general comprehension skill. *Journal of Experimental Psychology: Learning, Memory, and Cognition, 17*(2), 245-262.

Gernsbacher, M. A., & Varner, K. R. (1988). The multi-media comprehension battery [Tech. Rep. No. 88-3]. Eugene: University of Oregon. Retrieved from http://psych.wisc.edu/lang/materials/CompBat.html

Ginns, P. (2005). Meta-analysis of the modality effect. *Learning and Instruction, 15*, 313-331.

Gyselinck, V., Jamet, E., & Dubois, V. (2008). The role of working memory components in multimedia comprehension. *Applied Cognitive Psychology, 22*(3), 353-374.

Maki, W., & Maki, R. (2002). Multimedia comprehension skill predicts differential outcomes of web-based and lecture courses. *Journal of Experimental Psychology: Applied, 8*(2), 85-98.

Moreno, R. (2006). Does the modality principle hold for different media? A test of the method-affects-learning hypothesis. *Journal of Computer Assisted Learning, 22*(3), 149-158.

Schnotz, W. (2005). An integrated model of text and picture comprehension. In R. E. Mayer (Ed.), *The Cambridge handbook of multimedia learning* (pp. 49-69).

Shute, V. J., & Gawlick-Grendell, L. A. (1994). What does the computer contribute to learning? *Computers in Education, 23*, 177-186.

Sweller, J., Merrienboer, J., & Paas, F. (1998). Cognitive architecture and instructional design. *Educational Psychology Review, 10*(3), 251-296.

4 Digital Portfolio Use as a Growth Mindset Tool

Susan Hopper

Introduction

Digital portfolio use in the classroom demonstrates student growth over time and has been shown to be a valuable form for reflection. Studies concur that the combination of digital portfolios and thinking skills is powerful in measuring learning and achievement (Wall, 2006). Possible advantages of digital portfolios as studied by the Quebec Education Program (Abrami & Barrett, 2005) suggest portfolios involve students in the learning process, allow students to increase their ability to self-evaluate, teach students to make choices, promote feedback in the learning process, and allow students to reflect on their procedures, strategies, strengths, and weaknesses. Successfully using digital portfolios require students to practice critical thinking. The ability to assess one's own reasoning is fundamental in critical thinking. To reason well, students need to know they are using information in thinking. The information they are using must be accurate for reasoning to improve (Elder & Paul, 2008).

Unfortunately, schools often fall short of systematically teaching critical thinking, resulting in students leaving educational institutions without the ability to reason well through complex issues, to reason through subjects that have been their focus of learning, or think logically (Elder & Paul, 2008). Art Costa, co-author of *The School as a Home for the Mind* (2007) writes, "Although they may have completed 16 years…of formal education, they have not learned how to actively engage in the learning process. They have not developed skillful thinking habits" (…or more). While the use of digital portfolios gives students the opportunity to develop thinking skills, the use of digital portfolios combined with the systematic teaching of thinking skills would be much more effective.

Carol Dweck, a leading psychologist professor at Stanford University and author of *Mindset,* has researched student motivation and developed the theory that two types of learners exist. Students with a 'fixed mindset' want to appear to be smart. They lack effort and care more about other people's perception that they are smart, rather than possesing a real desire to learn. Students who believe they can learn through effort and education have a 'growth mindset.' They take on challenges and learn from mistakes. Growth mindsets alter the capacity to learn (Dweck, 2006). This paper will review literature on critical thinking aspects of digital portfolios and the intervention of pre-teaching growth mindsets, prior to implementing digital portfolios in the classroom to explore the possibility that growth mindset learning can transform the digital portfolio into a growth mindset tool.

Digital Portfolios

Portfolios were first used by artists, engineers, and architects to provide a visual representation of one's work and demonstrate skills. The early paper portfolios contained loose papers and drawings arranged in notebooks or folders. Introduced into education in the early 1990's, manual portfolios typically contained a collection of student writing. With the integration of technology into K-12 education, the purpose and design of portfolios have changed. A basic definition of a digital portfolio is "a purposeful collection of student work that illustrates effort, progress, and achievement in one or more areas" (Paulson, Paulson & Meyer, 1991). Digital portfolios have been used in schools as a form of assessment and reflective thinking, and as a means of monitoring a student's own learning (Abrami & Barrett, 2005).

Without a specific purpose, a portfolio is simply a folder of student work. Portfolios with different purposes result in various outcomes (Arter, Spandell, 1992) and can reinforce learning, act as an assessment tool, or support employment. Three common types of portfolios are working portfolios, display portfolios, and assessment portfolios. A working portfolio includes completed projects or student work that is in progress. Display portfolios showcase examples of the student's finest work; and assessment portfolios are used to exhibit student work to demonstrate accomplishment of specific learning goals (Barrett, 2005). Portfolio projects utilize technology to serve as a tool to capture the essence of the student and may include video clips, digital images, scanned documents, hyperlinks, journals, and digital storytelling. For the purpose of this paper, a digital portfolio is used for students as a personal learning environment to store work, facilitate student reflection, and demonstrate growth over time.

Studies concur that the combination of digital portfolios and thinking skills is a powerful measure of learning and achievement (Wall, 2006). Research has shown many advantages to the use of digital portfolios as a form of assessment. Digital portfolios provide a variety of pedagogical advantages, including serving as an assessment tool, offering a student-centered approach, promoting learning through problem solving, developing student reflection and critical thinking, and offering responsibility for learning content area skills and knowledge (Arter, 1995).

Digital portfolios are growth tools for both students and teachers. "Student and faculty portfolios are two sides of the same process because they facilitate reflection, innovation, and continuous quality of improvement in the classroom" (Wright, Knight, & Pomerleau, 1999). Teacher portfolios are used as a starting point for pedagogical development by concentrating attention on practice and reflection of practice (Tolsby, 2000). The main goal of a teacher portfolio is to use it as a tool to reflect on one's own teaching. Doolittle (1994) defines teacher portfolios as a self-reflection and meriting tool. "The portfolio provides a vehicle for assessing the relationship between a teacher's choices and or actions and their outcomes." Evidence shows that **digital portfolios** with multiple supports are beneficial to teacher reflection and **professional development**. The National Normal University in Taipei, Taiwan, found indications that teacher learning improved after using portfolios. In a six-month study of 44 in-service elementary teachers with 6.5 years average teaching experience, mixed-methods research practices were used to collect and analyze data on the process of constructing and using a digital portfolio. "Use of multiple supporting measures such as guided journal writing, discussion forum, and mechanisms of self and peer assessments enhance the role of the e-portfolio system as a mediator for converging and realizing the professional development of teachers (Sung, 2009)."

Pre-K through 6th grade teachers involved in the Newcastle University Digital Portfolio Project tackled the task of producing, storing and accessing assessment portfolios of learner's work using information and communication technology. Each of the 14 teacher-led case studies approached the project differently, resulting in a variety of end products; however, the value placed on using portfolios as a reflection tool and celebrating children's learning was a commonality among all the groups (Wall, 2006).

Growth Mindset

Digital Portfolios can help teachers improve their practice and provide a form of student reflection. Identified in the American Psychological Association (APA) report (1997), "successful learners are active, goal-directed, self-regulating and assume personal responsibility for contributing to their own learning" (p.7). For students to take ownership of their learning, they need opportunities to do so (Reynolds, 2006). Research indicates that the implementation of digital portfolios allows students to think critically, and become active, independent and self-regulated learners (Mills-Courts & Amiran, 1991). The process of reflection is what makes portfolios a tool for growth and not merely a collection of work (Foote & Vermette, 2001). Learners may analyze their own work and adjust goals as a result of reflection. Considerable research into 'thinking about thinking' or metacognition, suggests that deliberate teaching on the *process of learning* as well as the curriculum content should be taught (Berardi-Coletta, 1995). Costa and Kallick suggest skillful thinking is a set of habits of mind that must be cultivated and practiced (Costa & Kallick, 2007). Dweck's research concludes, "People with growth mindsets believe that they can learn, change, and develop needed skills. They are better equipped to handle inevitable setbacks, and know that hard work can help them accomplish their goals." Students with a fixed mindset believe that qualities of intelligence are fixed and cannot be developed therefore they respond differently from students with a growth mindset in learning situations (Dweck, 2006). The table below summarizes the differences between a growth mindset and a fixed mindset.

Table 1. Differences between the fixed mindset and the growth mindset (Visser, 2011).

Characteristics	Fixed Mindset	Growth Mindset
Belief	Capabilities are primarily seen as inborn talents which are hardly changeable	Capabilities are seen as mutable by effort and effective learning strategies
Tendency	To try to appear as capable as much as possible	To try to learn and improve as much as possible
Challenges	Are avoided because, in case of failure, they can give an impression of lack of talent	Are embraced because you can learn from them and they can lead to growth
View on effort	Is seen as an indication of a lack of talent	Is seen as a normal and necessary step to growth
Response to adversity or failure	Is seen as an indication of a lack of talent. Often leading to giving up early	Is seen as an indication that more effort and/or better strategies are needed
Response to criticism	Self-defeating defensiveness: own mistakes are not recognized and admitted	Inquisitive and interested, eager to learn and open to feedback and suggestions
View on success of others	Is seen as a threat because these other people might be viewed as more talented	Is seen as inspirational because lessons can be drawn from it for further learning
Impact on own development	Potential is under-utilized which is seen as a confirmation of one's own fixed mindset	Potential is developed which is a confirmation of one's growth mindset
Effect on other people	Can impede cooperation, feedback, and growth	Can invite cooperation, feedback and tips and stimulate growth

Motivational factors influence the use and growth of the ability for children to acquire new skills and knowledge and to transfer skills and knowledge to novel situations. Achievement motivation goals can be divided into two classes: learning goals and performance goals. Individuals try to increase their understanding or mastery of a topic using learning goals. With performance goals, individuals seek to gain positive judgments or avoid negative judgments of their competence. Research shows that the processes supporting learning goals focus on effort; whereas, with performance goals, the focus centers on ability. Further, this research shows that a focus on ability tends to cause individuals to withdraw from challenges, whereas a focus on progress through effort tends to cause individuals to seek challenges (Dweck, 1986). Studies suggest that when students believe their intelligence is fixed, it becomes critical for them to support their fixed ability through performance. When students think that they can increase their intellectual skills through effort, demonstrating a growth mindset, they become less concerned with the evaluation of their abilities and more concerned with long term cultivation of their skills (Blackwell, Dweck, & Trzesniewski, 2003).

Students need to be taught the importance of effort because affirming student's positive traits alone leads to a fixed mindset and a decline in motivation (Mueller & Dweck, 1998). As part of a developmental process, educators must teach intentionality and effort because students with a fixed mindset may embrace the unrealistic expectation that the mere existence of personal talents is enough to circumvent challenges (Dweck, 1998).

An interactive computer-based intervention called *Brainology* was developed to facilitate delivery of the growth mind-set to students. Students complete six modules where they learn how their brains work, visit the virtual brain lab, perform virtual brain experiments, view how the brain changes when they form new connections. Over time, they can become smarter. Students are taught how to apply the growth mindset concept to their schoolwork. In all studies, students who were taught the growth mindset skills outperformed the control groups. Teachers observed changes in performance of students in their desire to work harder and learn (Dweck, 2007).

Teaching students how to be skillful learners by developing a growth mindset before implementing digital portfolios may provide students with skills needed to be reflective thinkers, thereby creating the digital portfolio as a growth mindset tool.

Research Study
Pre-service teacher portfolio comparison

This study will incorporate pre-service teachers enrolled in a course of computers in the classroom, approximately 22 students per section, mostly sophomores and juniors. A requirement for the course is to create and present a digital portfolio as a final project. The hypothesis is that digital portfolios can be used to improve reflective and critical thinking based on the growth mindset training. The control group will use digital portfolios as a storage place for work. The treatment group will use digital portfolios as a growth mindset tool. The control and treatment group will take a pre-survey and a post survey to measure mindsets. The treatment group will be introduced to a growth mindset learning module prior to creating their portfolio. A rubric on reflective thinking will be distributed. Portfolio reflections of both groups will be assessed to determine quality of reflections. Pre-test and post-tests will be evaluated to determine attitudes toward a growth mindset.

Conclusion

The use of digital portfolios offers valuable opportunities to deepen student learning experiences through development of metacognitive skills such as goal setting, identifying strategies, and reflecting on one's learning, ultimately placing students at the center of his/her learning (Meyer, Abrami, Wade, & Deault, 2010). Growth mindset studies have shown students invest more in their learning by knowing that they can become smarter over time when their brains form new connections. Effort kindles their intelligence, producing growth, and they find new learning strategies in times of failure (Dweck, 2007). Students who develop a growth mindset will acquire skills to intuitively reflect on their work, appreciate and grow from feedback of others, and try different approaches to tackling challenges, which will enhance the effectiveness of digital portfolios as a growth mindset tool.

References

Abrami, P., & Barrett, H. (2005). Directions for research and development on electronic portfolios. *Canadian Journal of Learning and Technology, 31*, 3.

Arter, J. (1995). Portfolios for assessment and instruction. *ERIC Counseling and Student Services Clearinghouse, EDO-CG-95-10*, 0. Retrieved January 11, 2012 from the Eric database.

Arter, J., & Spandel, V. (1992). Using portfolios of student work in instruction and assessment. *Instructional Topics in Educational Measurement, 11*(1), 36-44.

Barrett, H. (2005). Researching electronic portfolios and learner engagement. *Canadian Journal of Learning and Technology, 31*(3), 48-55.

Berandi-Coletta, B., Buyer, L., Dominowski, R., & Rellinger, E. (1995). Metacognition and problem-solving: A process-oriented approach. *Journal of Experimental Psychology: Learning, Memory, and Cognition, 21*(1), 205-223.

Costa, A., & Kallick, B. (2008). *Learning And Leading With Habits of Mind*. Alexandria, VA.: Association for Supervision and Curriculum Development.

Costa, A. (2007). *The School As a Home for the Mind*. Thousand Oaks, CA.: Corwin Press.

Doolittle, P. (1994). Teacher portfolio assessment. *Eric AE digest, April*. Retrieved January 11, 2012, from http://www.ipm.edu.mo/update/intranet/dap/tt_hedu_evaluate/teaching/02.pdf.

Dweck, C. (2007). The perils and promises of praise. *Educational Leadership, 65*(2), 34-39. Retrieved October 19, 2011, from http://www.ascd.org/publications/educational-leadership/oct07/vol65/num02/The-Perils-and-Promises-of-Praise.aspx.

Dweck, C., Blackwell, L., & Trzesniewski, K. (2007). Implicit theories of intelligence predict achievement across an adolescent. *Child Development, 78*(1), 246-263.

Dweck, C. (2006). *Mindset: The New Psychology of Success*. New York, NY: Random House.

Dweck, C., & Mueller, C. (1998). Praise for intelligence can undermine children's motivation and performance. *Journal of Personality and Social Psychology*, *75*(1), 33-52.

Dweck, C. (1986). Motivational processes affecting learning. *American Psychologist*, *41*(10), 1040-1048.

Elder, L., & Paul, R. (2008). Critical thinking: The nuts and bolts of education. *Optometric Education*, *33*(3), 88-91.

Foote, C., & Vermette, P. (2001). Teaching portfolio 101: Implementing the teaching portfolio in introductory courses. *Journal of Instructional Psychology*, *28*(1), 31-37.

Meyer, E. , Abrami, P., Wade, A., & Scherzer, R. (2010). Electronic portfolios in the classroom: factors impacting teacher's integration of new technologies and new pedagogies. *Technology, Pedagogy and Education*, *20*(2), 191-207.

Mills-Court, K., & Amiran, M. (1991). Metacognition and the use of portfolios. *Portfolios process and product* (pp. 34-52). Portsmouth: Boynton/Cook Publishers Heinemann.

Paulson, F., Paulson, P., & Meyer, C. (1991). What makes a portfolio a portfolio? *Educational Leadership*, *February*, 60-63.

Principles work group. (n.d.). Learner-centered psychological principles: a framework for schools redesign and reform. *American Psychological Association*. Retrieved January 11, 2012, from www.apa.org/ed/governance/bea/learner-centered.pdf.

Reynolds, J. (2006). Learning-centered learning: A mindset shift for educators. *Inquiry*, *11*(1), 55-64.

Sung, Y., Chang, K., & Chang, T. H. (2009). Supporting teachers' reflection and learning through structured digital teaching portfolios. *Journal of Computer Assisted Learning*, *25*(4), 375-385.

Tolsby, H. (n.d.). Digital portfolio: A tool for learning, self-reflection, sharing and collaboration. *Avdeling for informasjonsteknologi - HÃ¸gskolen i Ã¸stfold* . Retrieved January 11, 2012, from http://www.ia.hiof.no/prosjekter/hoit/html/nr1_00/hakont.html.

Visser, C. (n.d.). Doing what works: forward in solution-focused change: developing a growth mindset - how individuals and organizations benefit from it. *Doing What Works: Forward in Solution-Focused Change*. Retrieved October 19, 2011 from http://solutionfocusedchange.blogspot.com/2011/06/developing-growth-mindset-how.html.

Wall, K. (2006). Investigating how digital portfolios can facilitate pupil talk about learning. *Technology, pedagogy, and education*, *15*(3), 261-273.

5 Use of Visual and Multimedia Resources in an Undergraduate Classroom: A Case Study

Krystyna K. Matusiak

Introduction

This paper focuses on the use of visual and multimedia resources for teaching and learning in an academic environment. The development of digital technologies and the growth of the Internet have enabled quick reproduction of information and its global distribution, and have led to the proliferation of information resources, available in a greater variety of types, formats and modes of representation. Such explosive growth of information and easy access to it is unprecedented in human history. It has dramatically changed an educational landscape and contributed to the resurgence of resource-based learning (Hill and Hannafin, 2001). Digital technology provided access to a greater amount and variety of educational resources, offered new ways of discovery, interaction, and experimentation, but also posed new challenges for instructional design and their integration into teaching. The digital transformation, however, is not only associated with the exponential growth of information, but also with multiple modes of knowledge representation, and especially with the emergence of the image as the dominant mode of representation. Digital technology is not solely responsible for creating the culture dominated by images and multimedia, but it has accelerated the cultural processes that began with photography, film, and television. Mitchell (1994) describes this shift in paradigm from textual to visual as a "pictorial turn." Recent advancements in computer graphics and the ease of publishing images on the Web have quickly changed the promise of a pictorial turn into reality. Digital technology has brought pictures to the forefront and placed them at the heart of the revolution in the production and dissemination of knowledge (Lukesh, 2002).

The explosion of visual and multimedia resources is not only a popular culture phenomenon (Felton, 2008). The influx of resources in multiple modes of representation creates a new potential for teaching and learning in an academic environment, which has been traditionally dominated by textual resources. Researchers emphasize the benefits of teaching and learning with visual materials and call for their wider adoption in an academic classroom (Carney & Levin, 2002; Felton, 2008; Mowat, 2002). As Elkins (2007) points out, "images are central to our lives, and it is time they become central in our universities" (p. 8). Jewitt (2006) stresses the multimodal nature of digital resources and argues for rethinking learning as a linguistic accomplishment. This dramatic shift from textual to visual and multimedia resources in academic environment raises important questions about instructional design and the ways students learn with resources in multiple modes of representation.

The emerging digital technologies with the abundance of visual and multimedia resources offer students new potentials for engagement and multiple paths into content (Hill and Hannafin, 2000; Jewitt, 2006). Empirical research, however, focused on the actual use of digital resources in higher education is relatively new. The information landscape is constantly evolving and offering new resources and new ways of interaction. This study contributes to this growing area of research through a case study by examining the use of digital resources in a large undergraduate classroom, assuming a contextual approach, and providing in-depth description of students' experiences in the natural academic setting.

The Study

The purpose of this case study was to explore students' use and perceptions of digital resources for academic work in the midst of the rapidly changing information environment. The focus of the study was on the use of visual and multimedia resources in specific class contexts, such as lectures, discussion sections, and students' projects and assignments. The notion of educational digital resources includes objects in digital libraries as well as information materials available on the open Web. The study addressed the following research questions: What types of digital resources do students encounter in the classroom and in their academic research? What are students' experiences in using the resources in multiple modes of representation?

Methodology

The study was designed as a qualitative case study. The emphasis was on users of digital information resources and their experiences and perceptions. Since this type of inquiry assumes an interpretive approach to the study of human behavior and attempts to make sense of phenomena in terms of the meanings people bring to them, the researcher decided to select qualitative methodology as an overall research strategy (Patton, 2002). The decision to choose qualitative methodology was also determined by the researcher's intention to present the findings in a descriptive form and to capture participants' voices. The case study approach helped to concentrate the research in a specific environment and establish the boundaries for the study.

A lower-level undergraduate geography class at a US Midwestern university was selected for the study. The selection of the class was purposeful, as it represented information-rich case, characterized by extensive use of digital materials in the classroom. As Stake (2008) notes, selection of an instrumental case implies a purposeful sampling of an environment where phenomena critical to the research purpose occur naturally. Digital resources have become ubiquitous on college campuses, but individual courses vary in which and how much digital technology is employed in the classroom due to differences in subject matter, traditions in academic disciplines, and faculty preferences. The decision to choose geography students as study participants was based on prior research indicating that geography faculty and students are among the heaviest users of digital recourses (Borgman et al., 2005; Harley, 2006). The focus on the case, as opposed to random selection of undergraduate students, made it possible for the researcher to observe students in the context of their regular academic practices.

Multiple qualitative data collection techniques were used to provide a thorough examination of the phenomena under study and to ensure the standards of credibility and trustworthiness. Triangulation was achieved by using multiple sources of evidence. The data collection techniques included: a survey, field observations in the classroom, interviews, a questionniare, and documentary evidence.

The survey was administered at the beginning of the study to gather basic demographic data. Students' participation was voluntary. As Table 1 indicates 27% of the students participated in the survey.

Data Collection Technique	Number of Participants	Percentage of Class Population
Lower-Level Class (GEOG 110) – 243 students		
Survey	65	27%
Questionnaire	60	25%
Faculty and TAs interview	3	

Table 1: Number of participants in data collection activities.

Field observations represented tha major source of data. Fieldwork lasted one semester and consisted of 64 hours of observations. Document analysis allowed to extend the investigation of resources. This process included an examination of syllabi, assignments, PowerPoint slides, selected student papers, and digital materials available as part of the course management system. The questionnaire with five open-ended questions was administered at the end of the semester to gather students' opinions on their experiences in using digital resources. 25% of the students participated in the questionnaire (Table 1). Semi-structured interviews were conducted with the professor teaching the class and 2 teaching assistants to address the questions that arose during field observations and document analysis.

Data analysis was conducted as qualitative content analysis focusing on themes and patterns that emerged from the data collection. The study adopted an inductive approach to content analysis that involved open coding and discovering categories, patterns, and themes in the data (Strauss & Corbin, 1990). The analytical process was thoroughly grounded in the data and guided by the research questions. The NVivo software was used in all the phases of the coding. The results of data analysis provided a foundation for case description and reporting of interpretive findings.

Case Description

The class observed for the study, Geography 110 (GEOG 110): The World – Peoples and Regions was a large class with 243 undergraduate students. The class provided an introduction to cultural, political, economic, urban, and environmental geographies of major world regions, including Latin America, Africa, Europe, South Asia, and East Asia. The goal of the course was for students to apply "geographic concepts to identify and describe relationships between people and places" (GEOG 110 Course Syllabus). The course examined colonial legacies in Latin America and Africa, Islam and democracy in Southwest Asia and North Africa, environmental issues and cultural nationalism in Europe, and population issues and economic development in Asia. The focus was on the process of globalization and its effects on world regions.

The lectures were held in one of the largest lecture halls on campus. As Table 2 demonstrates, the majority of students taking this class were freshmen and sophomores (81%); juniors and seniors represented 19% of the class. Undergraduate students usually take an introductory GEOG 110 to fulfill their general education requirements. The students who participated in the survey represented 30 different majors, ranging from architecture and engineering to global studies, history, philosophy, psychology. The majority of students (69%) were of college age (18-21 years old), 23% were between 22 and 25 years old, and 8% were older than 26.

Student Status	Registered Students		Survey Participants	
	No. of Students	%	No. of Students	%
Freshman	95	39%	21	9%
Sophomore	103	42%	24	10%
Junior	29	12%	15	6%
Senior	16	7%	5	2%
Total	243	100%	65	27%

Table 2: Student status - GEOG 110.

A junior faculty member in the Geography Department taught the class. She had taught this course with the same team of teaching assistants in previous semesters. Although the instructor was able to reuse many of her materials, she was still putting a considerable amount of time and effort into selecting new resources, revising her PowerPoint slides, and adding more current materials. As she explained in the interview, course development was an ongoing process: "this is the third time I taught this class and it is a lot better than the first time, but still there are so many places that I feel I could use an image such and such or I could use an image from this particular time period" (Instructor A, Interview).Two teaching assistants, Ph.D. students in geography, assisted her in teaching the course. They were primarily responsible for leading discussion sections and helping with students' assignments.

The class represented a blended model of instruction with on-site lectures, consisting of face-to-face instruction accompanied by electronic slide presentations, and online components using D2L (Desire-To-Learn) course management software (see Figure 1). The lectures were held twice a week on Tuesday and Thursday morning. The lecture hall was equipped with information and communication technology consisting of the instructor's computer workstation, Internet connection, LCD projectors, and two large overhead screens. The instructor utilized technology available in the classrooms for presenting PowerPoint slides and connecting to the Internet. Throughout the week, students also met in smaller groups (15-20 students) for discussions with the teaching assistants. Figure 1 demonstrates the course design with the emphasis on the instructional components in specific class contexts.

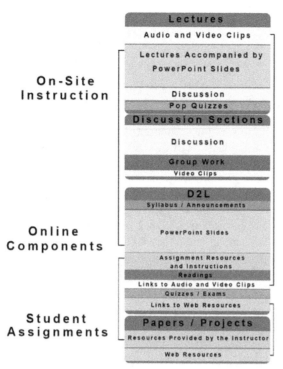

Figure 1: Course design in the contexts of lectures, discussion sections, and student assignments.

In addition to on-site lectures and discussion sections, the class also used D2L (Desire-To-Learn) course management software, provided by the university. D2L served as an important communication platform and a repository for all class materials. The instructor uploaded the slides before the lectures and encouraged students to make copies. Although some students found the class "very D2L influenced & dependent" (Student 29, Questionnaire), most of the questionnaire respondents indicated that they liked having D2L as a class component. Student 1 stated, "I check D2L frequently and appreciate classes that update often." Students liked the convenience of accessing materials online, "D2L has been helpful because it makes obtaining important papers + notes easier to get through with learning and allows us to get the resources that we need like articles or syllabuses" (Student 45, Questionnaire).

Despite the significant role that D2L played in class communication and providing access to resources, the lecture was the most important form of instruction. Every lecture began with a video clip and a brief discussion of a presented piece, followed by a PowerPoint presentation, projected onto two large screens. Occasionally, there would be some activities engaging students, such as a discussion of images or pop quizzes, but as the instructor acknowledged, the large size of the class and the lecture format made it impossible to introduce more participatory activities.

A few minutes before class, the instructor would play a video clip with a musical performance or a film. The class would start at 10:00 in the morning and, as students entered the lecture hall, they were surrounded by sounds of music from a country or region that was to be covered in the lecture. Video clips were projected onto the screens in the lecture hall. For example, for the lecture on South Africa students watched a musical performance of Miriam Makeba singing "Khawuleza." The instructor also presented the pictures of Miriam Makeba in PowerPoint (see Figure 2) and talked about her as a singer and anti-apartheid activist. The slide had several links to online resources about Miriam Makeba and her role as a civil rights activist.

As one of the students remarked: "video clips were great attention getters!" (Student 19, Questionnaire). The instructor intended not only to get students' attention, "literally wake them up," which was not a trivial factor in the morning lecture, but also to provide a contextual framework for the lecture topic and to raise students' awareness of the political and social conditions of a particular country or region. As she expressed in the interview, "I want them to come in and not just be in the lecture hall that is isolated from the rest of the world. I feel like they need to come in and see, oh there is something from somewhere else that is relevant to what we are going to be talking about, because I feel like this is part of setting the context" (Instructor A, Interview).

Figure 2: Slide with images of Miriam Makeba presented during lecture.

The video presentation and its discussion usually took about 5 minutes at the beginning of the class. Most of the class time was then devoted to a lecture accompanied by an electronic slide presentation projected on two screens. PowerPoint presentations accompanied all lectures. The instructor usually would show 20-30 slides per lecture. Slide presentations functioned like an aid to the lecture and a tool to display images and maps that are, as researchers point out, so critical to teaching geography (Borgman et al., 2005). The emphasis of PowerPoint was on visual elements. The instructor used text cautiously to introduce a topic or emphasize a point and used slides primarily for presenting images and maps. The images were selected purposefully to illustrate concepts, processes, or activities and were relevant to the lectures' content.

As the instructor explained in an interview, she tried to structure her lectures around "a big question", such as: "Is Islam compatible with democracy?" or "Why is Africa plagued by ethnic violence?" She then used PowerPoint slides with maps and images to explore multiple aspects of the issue. The images, included in the PowerPoint presentations, often depicted young people in other countries. The instructor admitted that she made a conscious effort to select images that could relate directly or personally to college age students: "I keep trying to include things that show students here what's going on for university students at other places; if you were there, your life might be different, so understand social conditions that they are operating in" (Instructor A, Interview).

The lectures, as well as some of the discussion sections, also included explicit discussions of the role of visual representations, especially of media coverage, in creating perceptions of other cultures. During lectures, the instructor tried to demonstrate how images influence our understanding of other countries and regions. In the lecture on Turkey, she posed a question on how Western images of the Middle East are informed and presented not only photos of women in traditional dress with covered heads, but also images of bustling city life, of nightlife in Istanbul, and of women in modern dress. She tried to provide sources that would dispel stereotypical or even negative imagery that is prevalent in popular media.

For assignments, students had to write six short two-to-three page essays, responding to class readings and other materials. The goal for essay assignments was to "develop critical thinking skills, prepare for discussion section, and assist in preparing for exams" (Course Syllabus). The topics, as well as all research resources, were specified on assignment sheets provided through D2L. For the first assignment, for example, students had to view a 20-minute video on the Cofan tribe and read two BBC articles on oil drilling in Ecuador.

In the questionnaire, students reported that they used videos and news articles for writing essays and found them useful: "articles and videos helped me understand essays I had to write"(Student 2). The video on the Cofan tribe that students watched for the first assignment had an emotional impact on them, which was evident in the class discussion. The video stimulated the class debate and students often referred to it in their arguments. The TA grading the essays noticed that "the video had the largest impact" and added, "It definitely had a real emotive effect on them, this particular video, but they failed to contextualize within a larger significance of the events" (TA2, Interview). Students were also supposed to read two articles for this assignment, but they rarely mentioned them in class discussion.

The students' overall assessment of the class was positive and many took time to fill out the optional comments' section in the questionnaire where they noted "everything in this class was very helpful! ☺" (Student 18) or "this was a very good class and resources were well taken advantage of (Student 10). Students liked "a wide variety of sources of information that made finding information for this class easier" (Student 7) and felt that "this class had a lot of resources available to help you with homework, quizzes, and exams" (Student 42). They noticed not only a wide variety of sources, but also multiple formats that, in their opinion, made learning easier. One student commented, "any learning process that involved more than just reading, like watching a video, obviously listening to audio, and discussing it was extra helpful" (Student 12).

Findings and Results

This section supplements the case description by presenting interpretive findings and results. The notion of resources and their relationship to teaching and learning practices were central to the inquiry. The empirical evidence gathered through this study allowed the researcher to examine the use of digital resources in the class contexts and to trace the relationship between the type of resources, their mode of representation, and students' activities.

Students in the geography class observed for this study encountered a wide variety of resources in the classroom and in their independent research and learning. They interacted predominantly with resources in the digital format that appeared in multiple modes, including visual, textual, and multimedia. The term mode refers to the way information is represented while multimedia is used according to Mayer's definition and implies a combination of modes and modalities, which may include spoken word, text, visuals, music, movement, etc. (Mayer, 1997). Resources often merged and overlapped, making a precise classification difficult. In the course of one lecture, students could be introduced to video clips, maps and images delivered through PowerPoint, and maps and images that were part of a website launched during lecture.

Students appreciated a wide selection of resources and use of them in combination. One of the students noted the variety of materials including "the PowerPoint, maps, videos, images, practically everything we used in class or online" (Student 18, Questionnaire), while another commented on the multimodal nature of resources to which they were exposed in this class: "PowerPoint and films incorporated looking at what we're learning about, hearing what we're learning about and applying it to the way we took in the information through multiple sources" (Student 12, Questionnaire).

Maps, images, and charts were featured prominently in lectures, which comes as no surprise and is consistent with the findings of other studies (Borgman et al., 2005). Geography instructors tend to supplement their lectures with maps and images to provide visual representation of places, people, and cultures. The surprising finding of this study is, however, the sheer amount of resources in multiple modes and the dominance of the visual mode in lectures. Video and audio clips were presented in every lecture and were also used occasionally in discussion sections. Students also used visual and multimedia resources when preparing for the assignments.

The distribution of resources by type and mode, however, varied and depended on the context of use (see Table 3). Visual resources dominated lecture presentations in the classroom, but students relied more heavily on textual materials in their independent work while preparing assignments and studying for exams. The analysis of context of use and students' perceptions and experiences also indicates that visual, textual, and multimedia resources played different roles in teaching and learning.

The concept of literacy practices proved to be very useful in analyzing the relationships between digital resources and students' learning activities. The use of resources was examined in selected students' practices in the specific contexts of the class (see Table 3). The concept of literacy practices represents a basic unit of the social theory of literacy that views literacy as a social practice (Barton & Hamilton, 2000). Literacy practices involve participants, activities, settings, artifacts, such as texts and technologies. Literacy practices in an academic setting represent students' ways of learning in a specific class contexts and are characterized by a distinctive sense of purpose. Practices consist of a number of activities and involve interaction with different types of resources.

Context of Use	Resource Type	Mode of Representation	Student Activities
Lectures	**Practice: Note Taking**		
	Lecture delivered by the instructor; PowerPoint slides; images; maps; charts;	Verbal/Oral Visual + text; Visual	Listening Reading Writing Looking Interpreting images
	Video clips	Multimedia	Watching Listening
Discussion Sections	**Practice: Group Preparation for Class Discussion**		
	PowerPoint slides; Images; maps; charts; Journal articles; Video and audio clips; Video films	Verbal Visual + text Text Multimedia	Listening Looking Writing Talking Watching
Projects and Assignments	**Practice: Writing Papers**		
	Journal articles; News articles; Websites; Video films	Text Visual + text Visual + text Multimedia	Reading Writing Watching
Online Quizzes in D2L	**Practice: Reviewing Class Material**		
	Student notes PowerPoint slides Textbook	Text Visual + text Text + visual	Reading Writing

Table 3: Examples of students' literacy practices in the context of use.

Table 3 indicates the relationship between resources, their mode of representation, and students' activities in selected literacy practices. Note taking during lectures, group work in preparation for class discussion, writing papers, and reviewing class materials for online quizzes are examples of students' literacy practices. It is necessary to emphasize here that the four practices described in Table 3 represent only a sample that was useful for analyzing the use of resources in class contexts and in connection with the mode of representation and students' activities.

The analysis of resources by mode of representation indicates the dominance of the visual mode in lecture presentations. Visual resources were used predominantly when students were introduced to new material. Images displayed in the PowerPoint presentations had primarily a descriptive function and were used to introduce new concepts, represent spatial relationships, and convey detailed information about subjects, regions, and countries under study. As Messaris (1994) argues, pictorial representation is based on the "conventions that provide the viewer with information similar to that typically used in real world perception" (p. 60). Therefore, images are useful in teaching subjects, such as geography, where reality of other worlds needs to be represented. Images are capable of expressing instantly an enormous amount of information and of remarkable range that otherwise would be very difficult to capture in words.

The use of images met with an overall approval from students. In response to the question posed in the questionnaire – "What resources, presented as part of this course, made the biggest impression on you and why?" – students emphasized the impact of visual and multimedia resources. Student 50 commented: "the PowerPoint presentations, video clips, articles, [I] like these sources because they give information visually," while Student 56 noted "[I prefer] video clips, PowerPoint, images. Visually seeing something that we're learning about is more compelling." Some students expanded on the role of PowerPoint slides and visual materials in the learning process: "PowerPoint during class is huge because I'm a visual learner" (Student 20, Questionnaire). This comment was echoed by Student 59: "all of the PowerPoint presentations provided in class helped out greatly. I'm a visual learner so it was great to see this way of learning was provided" (Questionnaire).

Students' comments point out yet another important role of visuals in learning. Images served as mnemonic aids and helped them recall lecture materials better. One of the students observed that visual resources help in learning and assist in remembering: "Images and PowerPoint presentations make the biggest impression on me because they are visual and catch my attention. They make things easier to remember" (Student 3, Questionnaire).

The prevalent use of images and their important descriptive and mnemonic functions emerge as important themes in this case study. However, the findings indicate also the constraints of using visual resources as instructional tools. The detailed analysis of specific class contexts (see Table 3) demonstrates that resources in a visual mode of representation were rarely used alone, without a verbal or textual explanation. In most situations, a visual mode was combined with a linguistic mode, either in the form of a verbal presentation during lectures or in a variety of textual forms. The use of textual resources increased when students had to prepare for quizzes or exams and worked on papers. In the contexts when students had to analyze or synthesize knowledge the role of images diminished while a distinct role of language as the system for the representation of argument became evident.

The limited role of images as a analytical tool in academic discourse was acknowledged by the instructor of the observed class, who despite using a variety of images, was not always satisfied with her selection: "I try in my lectures to tell the story, but sometimes I find it really hard because you know the stories get complicated and sometimes it's very difficult to come up with an image" (Instructor A, Interview). Although images are unparalleled in the descriptive function, they generally lack an ability to present a point of view, or to negate or affirm a statement: in other words, they are not good tools for analysis and academic discourse. As Messaris (1994) argues, "mages are 'deficient' in a more general sense as vehicles of analytical communication."

While visual resources featured prominently in lectures, multimedia played a secondary role. They were also used occasionally in discussion sections and as research material for written assignments. The use of videos was complemented by news articles and classroom discussion, and often required an additional explanation from the instructor. As noted in the case description, videos had an emotional impact on students and contributed to the students' increased interest in the topic, but not necessarily to its better understanding. The use of video for the written assignment on oil drilling in Ecuador is an example of the challenges of using multimedia as a source material for written assignments. The video on the Cofan tribe made a strong impression on students, but their emotional reaction did not translate into a persuasive argument in writing. One could argue that this example demonstrates the limitations of multimedia and the difficulty in navigating between modes. However, this was an isolated case in the study and further research is required to draw more general conclusions.

This study demonstrates that the visual mode of representation is, indeed, gaining importance in the digital environment. Students in the class examined for this study were exposed to a wide variety of resource types in multiple modes, including images, maps, journal articles, datasets, video and audio clips, news sites, and educational and commercial websites. The classroom environment was truly multimodal and often required students to navigate and translate between modes of representation.

Discussion

As the case description and the analysis of results indicate, lecture presentations in the class observed for the study prominently featured visual resources and multimedia. Images and maps were used to introduce students to new material, explain concepts, and provide visual representation of places, people, and cultures. It is true that the subject matter in geography lends itself to the use of visual materials, but the sheer amount of images in the observed class confirms the prediction of many scholars about the "pictorial turn," a shift in paradigm from textual to visual (Lukesh, 2002; Mitchell, 1994).

The abundance of visual resources was evident in the class observed in this study and met with students' expectations and preferences. Many study participants described themselves as "visual learners" and believed that they benefited from the instruction with visual materials. Educational psychology research examining the relationship between cognitive styles and mode of presentation in learning actually supports those claims (Mayer, 1997, 2005; Riding & Douglas, 1993). Mayer (2005) argues that presenting material in verbal and visual modes allows instructors to take advantage of the full capacity of learners' cognitive processing. Empirical research examining the multimedia theory is inconclusive with some studies demonstrating the benefits of learning with images (Carney & Levin, 2002; Mayer & Gallini, 1990; Mayer, 2005) and others indicating that there is no significant improvement in student performance (Rasch & Schnotz, 2009).

Cognitive processing, however, represents only one of the factors that contribute to effective learning. In addition, students' attitudes are affected by other motivational, social, and cultural factors, including the information environment that is increasingly becoming more visual. Although these factors will not fundamentally change the human cognitive system, they influence students' expectations, perceptions, and information habits. Nonetheless, cognitive research on the impact of resource mode on knowledge construction is critical and represents an area that requires more investigation, especially in light of students' preferences and the increased use of visual materials in instruction.

The analysis of students' stated preferences indicated a general positive perception of the use of visual resources for teaching and learning. The investigation of students' practices, however, demonstrated that the use of visual resources was not uniform across class contexts. The distribution of resources by mode depended on class context. Visual resources were used predominantly in lectures that introduced students to new topics; textual materials were used more extensively in student research and independent study. This observation supports cognitive psychology research on the benefits of using visual materials in contexts characterized by low prior knowledge, when students are introduced to new subjects (Mayer & Gallini, 1990; Schnotz; 2002).

Visual and linguistic resources not only were used in different class contexts, but also played distinct roles in knowledge construction. Resources in the linguistic mode were present in all contexts of use and gained increasing importance as students progressed throughout the course. They were used to present concepts and arguments, analyze information, and synthesize knowledge. Visual resources, on the other hand, were used mostly to introduce topics, describe new environments, and interpret concepts. Representative or interpretative functions of visual resources in teaching have been recognized by researchers, who note that an appropriate use of images not only makes lectures more attractive, but also enhances student learning (Carney & Levin, 2002; Mayer & Gallini, 1990; Mowat, 2002).

The descriptive function of images appears to be particularly important in light of Laurillard's approach to academic teaching as mediated learning. Laurillard (2002) argues that academic study is removed from experiential learning and represents a second-order experience. The knowledge that students gain is not acquired from direct experience, but instead is mediated by their teachers and augmented by the resources that provide a description of the worlds under study. As Messaris (1994) emphasizes, images have a unique ability to convey a tremendous amount of information instantly, and their descriptive power is unsurpassed. On the other hand, images have a limited capacity in analytic discourse and in making generalizations. In contexts where students had to present arguments and synthesize knowledge, they relied more on textual resources. Visual and textual resources therefore played complimentary, yet distinct functions.

As the findings of this study indicate, the use of visual resources in the classroom plays positive roles as it addresses the individual differences in students' cognitive styles, helps students remember the material, provides a rich description of the subjects under study, and meets students' expectations for a learning environment that is enhanced by technology. However, recognizing the benefits of images for students' learning does not automatically imply a pedagogic design dominated by visual materials. This study also points out the limitations of the visual mode and underscores the importance of the linguistic mode for academic learning.

This study demonstrates that the digital transition has led to a wider adoption of visual and multimedia resources for teaching and learning. Their use in an academic environment, however, is sometimes indiscriminate. The choice of mode of representation in the instructional design impacts practices in the classroom and the way student learn. An effective use of visual and multimedia resources for teaching and learning should carefully consider the mode of representation, type of resources, and their unique strengths as well as limitations in the context of specific academic practices.

Conclusion

This case study provided in-depth description of the use of digital resources in a specific classroom context of use. It demonstrated that digital technology not only enables wider access to information resources, but also increases the possibilities for knowledge representation while providing a greater variety of educational resources. The findings of the study indicate that the distribution of resources depends on the context of use and pointed to different roles of visual and multimedia resources in student academic practices.

Digital technology has enabled faster and easier creation and reproduction of visual and multimedia resources and their integration into the teaching and learning process. The proliferation of visual resources and multimedia in the digital environment and their increasing role in teaching and learning represents a new area of interdisciplinary research that deserves further attention.

References

Barton, D. & Hamilton M. (2000). Literacy practices. In D. Barton, M. Hamilton, & R. Ivanic (Eds.), *Situated literacies: Reading and writing in context* (pp. 7-15). London: Routledge.

Borgman, C.L., Smart, L., Millwood, K. A., Finley, J.R. Champeny, L., Gilliland, A.J., & et al. (2005). Comparing faculty information seeking in teaching and research. Implications for the design of digital libraries. *Journal of the American Society for Information Science and Technology.* 56(6), 636-657.

Carney, R. N. & Levin, J. R. (2002). Pictorial illustrations still improve students' learning from text. *Educational Psychology Review,* 14(1), 5-26.

Elkins, J. (2007). *Visual literacy.* New York: Routledge.

Felten, P. (2008). Visual literacy. *Change,* 40(6), 60-64.

Harley, D. (2006). *Use and users of digital resources: A focus on undergraduate education in the humanities and social sciences.* Berkeley, CA: Center for Studies in Higher Education. Retrieved November 3, 2008 from http://cshe.berkeley.edu/publications/publications.php?id=211

Hill, J. R., & Hannafin, M. J. (2001). Teaching and learning in digital environments: The resurgence of resource-based learning. *Educational Technology, Research and Development, 49*(3), 37-52.

Jewitt, C. (2006). *Technology, literacy and learning: A multimodal approach.* London: Routledge.

Laurillard, D. (2002). *Rethinking university teaching: A conversational framework for the effective use of learning technologies.* London: Routledge.

Lukesh, S. S. (2002). Revolutions and images and the development of knowledge: Implications for research libraries and publishers of scholarly communications. *Journal of Electronic Publishing, 7*(3). Retrieved October 25, 2011 from http://dx.doi.org/10.3998/3336451.0007.303

Mayer, R. E. & Gallini, J. K. (1990). When is an illustration worth ten thousand words? *Journal of Educational Psychology,* 82(4), 715-726.

Mayer, R. E. (1997). Multimedia learning: Are we asking the right questions? *Educational Psychologist,* 32(1), 1.

Mayer, R. E. (2005). Introduction to multimedia learning. In R.E. Mayer (Ed.), *The Cambridge handbook of multimedia learning* (pp. 1-16). New York: Cambridge University Press.

Messaris, P. (1994). *Visual literacy: Image, mind, and reality.* Boulder, CO: Westview Press.

Mitchell, W.J.T. (1994). *Picture theory.* Chicago, IL: The University of Chicago Press.

Mowat, E. (2002). Teaching and learning with images. *VINE,* 32(3), 5-13.

Patton, M.Q. (2002). *Qualitative research & evaluation methods* (3rd ed.). Thousand Oaks, CA: Sage Publications.

Rasch, T. & Schnotz, W. (2009). Interactive and non-interactive pictures in multimedia learning environments: Effects on learning outcomes and learning efficiency. *Learning & Instruction,* 19(5), 411-422.

Riding, R.J. & Douglas, G. (1993). The effect of cognitive style and mode of presentation on learning performance. *British Journal of Educational Psychology*, 63, 297-307.

Schnotz, W. (2002). Towards an integrated view of learning from text and visual displays. *Educational Psychology Review,* 14(1), 101.

Stake, R. E. (2008). Qualitative case studies. In N.K. Denzin & Y. S. Lincoln (Eds.), *Strategies of qualitative inquiry* (pp.119-149). Thousand Oaks, CA: Sage Publications.

Strauss, A., & Corbin, J. (1990). *Basics of qualitative research: Grounded theory procedures and techniques.* Newbury Park, CA: Sage Publications.

6 Computer Literacy Learning Emotions of ODL Teacher-Students

Hendrik D. Esterhuizen, A. Seugnet Blignaut, Christo J. Els & Suria M. Ellis

Introduction

Affective computing may solve emotion deficiency issues of novice and developing students in Open Distance Learning environments while they engage with new technologies for the first time. Affective computing relates to the role of affective experiences and the emotional expressions of people during their learning of skills essential for using computers and other electronic devices. In some cases, applications are taught to mimic human emotions in order to establish computer-human interaction (MIT Media Lab, s.a.), while others interact with information of facial expression in order to adjust teaching strategies to provide personalized learning environment (Chen & Luo, 2006). This paper does not relate to the computing strategies of affective communication, but with the affective experiences of developing learners about to experience their first e-learning environment.

Affective communication is communicated to someone (or something) either with or about affect. People communicate their affective experiences daily. Affective communication involving computers represents a vast, but largely untapped research area (MIT Media Lab, s.a.). It is not clear how computers contribute towards affective experiences of previous disadvantaged communities.

Teaching and learning use modern educational technologies to create an "ideal" learning environment by integrating information and communication technology into curricula. Learning environments not only embody the learning styles of students, but also reform traditional teaching structures and the essence of education. Affective experiences of learning environments can cause affiliation or separation among teachers and students, or students and students (Chen & Luo, 2006).

Literature Review

From the late 1950s into the 1970s, Krathwohl *et al.* (1973) have classified the domains of human learning. Bloom's well-known taxonomy of learning comprises cognitive learning (knowing), affective learning (feeling) and psychomotor learning (doing). The affective domain deals with things emotionally, such as feelings, values, appreciation, enthusiasms, motivations, and attitudes. Learning is enhanced through high self-esteem and low anxiety, having a positive attitude towards learning, it is shared through emotions, values and beliefs in a group where learning takes place from one another through active engagement. Learning with and from computers is greatly influenced by learners' perceptions on the usefulness of computers (Ingleton, 1999).

Affect includes aspects like emotion, mood, attitude and value (Jones, 2010). Interface design, the relationship between the user's attitude and emotions which could influence the user's motivation, should be taken into account (Chang, 2005). Failure to succeed in getting things right disheartens students. They should be made aware that emotions are a normal part of learning. Accurate identification of students' emotional and cognitive state is pivotal in support for successful learning (Kort *et al.*, 2001). Agyei and Voogt (2011) found that low teacher anxiety was the most important dimension of attitudes, and for teachers, competence is the strongest predictor of classroom integration of technology. Anderson (1996) developed a Computer Anxiety Rating Scale and found that previous computer experience is an important element of success in undergraduate courses in information systems. Computer anxiety is also implicated in performance, as is perceived ease of use and language ability (Conti-Ramsden *et al.*, 2010).

Introducing a computer literacy course enhanced students' computer and Internet self-efficacy. Computer literacy training also contributed towards positive attitudes towards computers and the Internet, while reducing students' computer anxiety. It produced positive responses regardless of students' prior ICT experience, though it enhanced computer self-efficacy, Internet self-efficacy and computer attitudes in the case of students with low prior ICT experience (Papastergiou, 2010). Moolman and Blignaut (2008) emphasize that e-learning for the individual user requires access to technology, computer literacy, self-discipline, the drive to develop and the confidence to use technology to achieve objectives. The digital divide is especially apparent in developing communities. Amidst calls to bridge this divide by introducing information technology to such communities, it could be rightly asked whether they have the discipline, motivation, and skills to learn by means of such a complex learning strategy. Variables such as gender, age and experience directly influence the intention to use technologies, as well as self-efficacy, anxiety and attitude (Verhoeven et al., 2010). Studies indicate that younger teachers tend to feel more positive with regard to teaching with technology and most probably would use it in instruction. Teachers just out of college display a higher level of confidence than their older peers (Christensen & Knezek, 2008).

Design and Methods

Study Context

The School of Continuing Teacher Education (SCTE) at the Potchefstroom Campus, North-West University (NWU), enrolls about 24 000 in-service teacher-students for *inter alia* the Advanced Certificate in Education (ACE) or the National Professional Diploma in Education (NPDE). The SCTE follows an open distance learning (ODL) model that aims to increasingly adopt learning technology for effective delivery of education to large numbers of unqualified and under-qualified teachers across the diverse population of South Africa. The concern is whether students from mostly disadvantaged communities are ready to engage with digital learning technologies. These qualification programs include basic computer-literacy components to prepare teacher-students for using computers as part of their teaching and learning. SITES 2006 (Second Information Technology in Education Study), a large scale international comparative study that focused on teachers' pedagogical use of computers in classrooms, indicated that less than 40% of South African schools were ready to use computers in teaching and learning, and that about a quarter of the teachers were able to use computers and other electronic devices in their classes. These figures indicate that teachers in general are not ready to engage with e-learning, in spite of the call from the e-Education White Paper that by 2013 all teachers and learners should be prepared to effectively use computers for pedagogical and administrative practices (South Africa, 2004) .

Method

This study followed a *Fully Mixed Sequential Equal Status* research design (Leech & Onwuegbuzie, 2009) with a two-phase qualitative analysis, followed by quantitizing of the qualitative data (Saldăna, 2009) in order to quantitatively validate the emotion codes that the researchers identified from the qualitative data. This design would enable researchers to construct a visual bi-directional model to readily depict the phenomenon of computer literacy learning emotions at a glance (Saldăna, 2009). The dataset contains the research participants' verbal responses to five open-ended items from a survey, based on Morris and de Nahlik's (2009) *Technology Acceptance Model (TAM)*. The instrument was designed for novice computer users from rural and disadvantaged communities in South Africa. The five-item dataset relates to (i) the challenges the participants experienced during computer literacy training; (ii) the influence of their background on their computer acceptance; (iii) their perceptions on the value of computer-literacy training they received; and (iv) the personal advantages of becoming computer literate.

The participants comprised N=339 teacher students, enrolled for either an ACE or NPDE qualification through ODL at the SCTE of the NWU during 2010. They have all previously been unsuccessful in completing a computer literacy module, and have presented themselves for computer-literacy training at learning centers across South Africa in order to improve their skills and pass the module. They all gave consent for the research and acknowledged that their participation was voluntary. The survey was completed during these computer-literacy training workshops. This purposive sample related to criterion-based selection of participants (Merriam, 1998) to create attributes essential to the purpose of the study, i.e. determining the *emotions* that teacher-students experience while *learning* with and about technology.

Qualitative Methods

Affective coding methods investigate subjective qualities of human experience (e.g., emotions, values, conflicts, judgments) by directly acknowledging and naming the experiences. *Emotion coding,* as a method of affective coding, taps into the inner cognitive systems of research participants by inferring to the feelings they experience. Emotion coding focuses on the analysis that judge the merit and worth of programs (Saldăna, 2009). This study accepts the definition of emotion as "an affective state of consciousness in which joy, sorrow, fear, hate, or the like, is experienced, as distinguished from cognitive and volitional states of consciousness" (Dictionary.com, 2011). Emotion cannot be separated from action as they are integrated in the same flow of events and the one leads into the other. Emotion coding provides insight into participants' perspectives, worldviews, life conditions, and it also influences learning (Saldãna, 2009).

Emotion coding is appropriate for qualitative studies that explore intrapersonal and interpersonal participant experiences and actions. A first cycle comprises emotion coding (Saldãna, 2009), and labels the feelings participants may experience and taps into the inner cognitive systems of participants: "[Emotion] is a feeling and its distinctive thoughts, psychological and biological sates, and range from propensities to act" (Goleman, 1995, p. 289). The verbal responses of the teacher-students to the five open-ended items constituted the integrated qualitative dataset on interpersonal and intrapersonal experiences and *emotions* while *learning* with and about the use of computers. Hundreds of words exist to describe human emotions—the repertoire of potential codes is therefore vast. The researchers used categorized lists of emotion to select descriptive words for creating appropriate codes for the analysis (Buddhamind.com, s.a.; Psychpage.com, 2010; Saldãna, 2009; Walter Hottinga.com, 2011).

To ascertain how the novice learners perceived their learning of new skills, a second cycle of coding followed according to the Jungian-inspired (Jung, 1990), *Conscious Competent Model*, outlining the four levels a person goes through when learning new skills and knowledge. They are (i) unconscious incompetent, (ii) conscious incompetent, (iii) conscious competent, and (iv) unconscious competent (Businessballs.com, 2010). The progression is from stage 1 through 2 and 3 to 4 and it is not possible to jump stages. For some skills, especially advanced ones, people can regress to a previous stage if they fail to practice and exercise their new skills.

The researchers used Atlas.ti™, a computer-based qualitative data analysis program, to analyze the qualitative sections of the data according to an open thematic approach (Anderson *et al.*, 2001). The analysis encompassed coding according to (i) a first phase emotion coding methodology, and (ii) a second phase coding relating to the four levels of the conscious competent learning model (Saldãna, 2009).

Quantitative Methods

The instances of qualitative understanding in terms of the two-cycle approach were exported to a spreadsheet and the data were checked for integrity. The spreadsheet listed 1235 instances of coding consisting of four variables for learning (conscious competent coding), and 31 emotion coding variables. Each instance contained two values: one for conscious competent coding, and one for the emotion coding. Three additional variables columns reflected a summary of the two-cycle coding: a single value representing conscious competent learning as a four-point scale, as well as a two-point scale value, each representing technophilia and technophobia calculated according to the conceptual analysis of the qualitative data. Validity, by means of factor analysis, was calculated on the data. A two-way cross-tabulation (contingency table) (Cramer & Howitt, 2004) displayed the interrelationship between emotion coding (technophilia and technophobia) and the stages of conscious competent learning.

Findings and Discussion of Findings

Quantitative Findings

Quantitative factor analyses were performed to calculate the validity of the 31 emotion codes (scales) that were identified from the qualitative analysis. Twenty seven scales (*successful, confident, reproach, powerless, expectant, appreciated, stimulated, uneasy, irked, encouraged, inferiority, apprehension, confused, lacking, fascination, involved, frustration, thankful, ashamed, optimistic, sharing, enthusiasm, pleased, dismay, touched, moved, acknowledge*) indicated a 1-factor loading, while two emotion scales (*enjoyment* and *despair*) indicated a two-factors loading. Validity was assumed for these emotion scales. The 1-factor loading of items (tags) on the majority of emotion scales (codes) indicated items load on single variables (1-factor loading), similar to the emotion code items (tags) identified by the researchers in the qualitative analysis, which therefore reflects the trustworthiness of the qualitative coding. The scale *idealized* indicated a three-factor loading. On closer examination of the scale *idealized*, it loaded with *despair* and *enjoy* as Factor 1; with *lacking* and *yearning* as Factor 2; and with *enjoy, despair, thankful* and *yearning* as Factor 3 (Table 1). The validity and findings pertaining to the scale *idealized* were interpreted with confidence despite its 3-factors loading, as they are valid in the specific mostly rural and disadvantaged context of the research participants who unconsciously enjoy acquiring benefits from the subsidized course, and the additional time and effort from lecturers and facilitators. As a result of their hopeless situation and previously disadvantaged background, they idealize technology as the answer to creating a better future. The scale *yearning* indicated a 5-factors loading. On closer examination, *yearning* loaded with *idealized* and *lacking* as Factor 2, with *enjoyment, despair, idealized* and *thankful* as Factor 3; with *reproach* as Factor 4; with *stimulated* as Factor

5; and with *fascination* as Factor 6 (Table 1). Because of its 5-factors loading, the findings regarding the scale *yearning* were interpreted with caution.

Table 1: Factor analysis of the Emotion Codes (≥ 2-factor loading)

Scales	F1	F2	F3	F4	F5	F6	F7	F8
Enjoyment	0.579		-0.435					
Despair	0.797		0.237					
Idealized	-0.224	0.203	-0.205					
Lacking		0.854						
Thankful			-0.803					
Yearning		-0.491	0.274	0.215	-0.249	0.300		
Reproach				-0.997				
Stimulated					0.980			
Fascination						-0.930		
Uneasy							0.790	
Irked							0.620	
Inferiority								0.719
Apprehension								0.699

As reported in Table 1, the initial scales *uneasy* and *irked* resulted in a combined 1-factor loading on factor seven (F7); as well as the initial scales *inferiority* and *apprehension* that resulted in a combined 1-factor loading on factor eight (F8). These findings were not surprising as during qualitative revision, a close resemblance was established between the data for *uneasy* and *irked,* and the data for *inferiority* and *apprehension.* The authors decided to group the initial scales *uneasy* and *irked* into the single scale *irked,* and *inferiority* and *apprehension* into a single scale *apprehension.*

Table 2: Cross tabulation between learning and Emotion Coding Variables

	Technophobia	Technophilia	Total
Unconscious and Conscious Incompetent	42.5%	35.1%	77.6%
Conscious and Unconscious Competent	2.2%	20.2%	22.4%
Total	44.7%	53.3%	

Variables for learning (*conscious competent coding*) and emotion coding (*technophobia* and *technophilia*) were correlated using cross tabulation (Table 2). Significant correlations were determined between variables using Cramer's effect size (V) (Ellis & Steyn, 2003). An effect size $V \leq 0.2$ is considered a small statistical effect with little or no practical significance. An effect size $0.3 \leq V \leq 0.4$ is considered a medium effect which tends towards a practically significant correlation, while affect size $V \geq 0.5$ is considered a large effect which indicates a practically significant correlation.

Table 2 indicates that of the total instances of *learning* and *emotion* variables, approximately the same proportion of respondents were technophobic and technophiliac, while 90% of the conscious and unconscious competent respondents were technophiliac. A medium effect ($V = 0.378$, $p < 0.01$) which tends towards a practically significant correlation, was found between these learning and emotion variables. These findings indicate instances of incompetence related to comparable numbers of technophilia and technophobia. However, with increased competence, technophobia almost disappears and technophilia increases. Surprisingly enough, more incompetence than competence relates to technophilia. This seemingly contradictive finding could possibly be ascribed to the so called Dunning-Kruger (1999) effect in psychology—a cognitive bias in which unskilled people make poor decisions and reach erroneous conclusions, but their incompetence denies them the metacognitive ability to appreciate their mistakes. The unskilled consequently suffer from illusory superiority, while the highly skilled underrate their abilities, suffering from illusory inferiority.

No practically significant correlations were found between the n = 29 emotion codes in the quantitative dataset. However, as reported in Table 3, a medium effect size ($V = 0.39$, $p < 0.01$) which tends toward a practically significant correlation, was calculated between the emotion code successful and competence in respondents who were technophiliac (Table 3), whereas 27.2% of the competent group experienced the emotion of feeling successful versus 1.6% of the incompetent group.

Table 3: Cross-tabulation between the emotion code successful and competent for technophiliac respondents

	Successful		Totals
	Unsuccessful	Successful	
Incompetent	62.4%	1.0%	63.4%
Competent	26.6%	10.0%	36.6%
Totals	89.0%	11.0%	100.0%

Table 4 shows cross-tabulation between different levels of competence and technophobia and technophilia. The findings of this table are used in the conclusion and recommendation section to develop a *Model for Computer Literacy Learning Emotions* (V=0.484, p < 0.01).

Table 4: Cross-tabulation between different levels of competence and technophobia and technophilia

	Unconscious Incompetent	Conscious Incompetent	Conscious Competent	Unconscious Competent	Totals
Technophobia	27.0%	15.7%	1.8%	0.2%	44.7%
Technophilia	10.2%	26.0%	9.6%	9.5%	55.3%
Totals	37.2%	41.7%	11.4%	9.7%	100%

Qualitative Findings

The quantitative analyses validated 29 qualitative codes (Table 5). Two themes emerged from the emotion coding of the teacher-students' experiences with personal computers, the Internet, mobile phones, or other new mobile learning devices: (i) *technophilia*: teacher-students experiencing a strong enthusiasm for advanced technology (Figure 1); and (ii) *technophobia*: teacher-students suffering from an irrational fear or dislike for advanced technology (Figure 2). These themes included categories of codes relating to the affective experiences of developing learners communicated with or about affect in response to the open ended questions about using computers.

Technophilia

The teacher-students' affinity for learning with, and learning from technology presented four categories ranging from the *promised* they expressed on what technology could bring to them, *desire* to learn with technology, the ability to *engaged* with technology, and finally being *grateful* for the advances of technology. The teacher-students expressed strong positive desires and intentions to master new competencies once their limitations of access to technology dissipated (Figure 1).

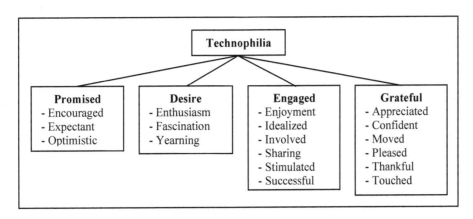

Figure 1: Emotion Coding Themes and Codes Structured as Technophilia

Technophobia

The theme technophobia related to the teacher-students' expressed feelings of dependence on being assisted due to their anxiety while using new technologies. From the analysis, three categories emerged capturing the technophobic experiences of the teacher-students: *embarrassed, afraid* and *inadequacy* (Figure 2).

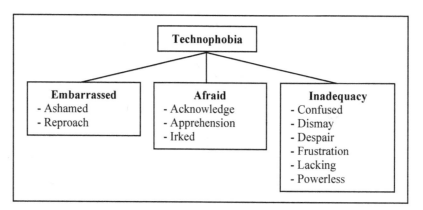

Figure 2: Emoting Coding Themes and Codes Structured as Technophobia

Table 5: Emotion Codes, Learning Codes, Descriptions and Typical Quotations

Code and Description	Quote
Emotion Codes	
Acknowledge Accept or admit the existence or truth	*It was difficult for me to hold the mouse as I was shaking ... But I made it and passed*
Appreciated Recognizing the full worth	*From the start I had difficulties in holding my mouse and starting my computer. After assistance I totally enjoyed it because my teachers assisted me well. Thanks*
Apprehension Anxious or fearful that something bad or unpleasant will happen	*In the beginning before I enrolled I was computer illiterate. After enrolling I can use computers though I am still struggling with some aspects*
Confident Feeling or showing certainty about something	*I started to read the study guide for end-user computing for educators. That is where I get more information about computers. I learned the parts of the computer*

Code and Description	Quote
Confused Unable to think clearly or act with understanding	*With the information that I now have I'm more than motivated to come closer to computers*
Despair Feeling of complete loss of hope	*The problem I experienced in passing my computer literacy is I don't have computer skills. I also don't have a computer to practice*
Dismay Losing enthusiasm and becoming disillusioned	*I was sometimes slow to complete the task because it was the first time for me to use a computer*
Encouraged Promoted, advanced, or fostered	*Because I have realized the importance of using a computer in my classroom for many task e.g. set question papers, making class tests and recording marks for assessment*
Enjoyment Receive pleasure and satisfaction	*I like to use a computer; it makes my work to be very neat and beautiful. I will encourage my children and the community to use computers to make their life easier*
Enthusiasm Excitement or interest	*I can walk tall and people were amazed that we have been given a chance to do this*
Expectant The prospect of overcoming barriers	*We are living in a technological world, so computer knowledge is a must to all, especially educators* *Being computer literate will help us to gain access to more information from all over the world*
Fascination An intense interest	*I have charged my mind, I am very interested in computer, in so much that I want to buy it and use it at my home*
Frustration Feeling of being upset or annoyed, especially because of inability to change or achieve something	*In my opinion I think this is the simplest module of them all, since its practices are for daily life or experience. The problems might be studying the module without having a computer, or practicing it*
Idealizing Regard as perfect or better than in reality	*I have never experienced any problem in passing the module on computer literacy but I teach at a farm school where there are no computers. Using a computer for the first time may be a problem but I am interested in knowing the basics of the computer*
Involved Becoming interested and enjoy	*I used computers during my studying with the NWU and became very interested. As from now, I will never look back I am going to use a computer in everything that needs to be done*
Irked Irritated; annoyed	*The main problem is that we, most people, do not have access to computers. If we all have computers just like televisions at home or school, the module would have been no problem. I would have been better skilled. Having no clear idea of the way the computer functions was the other main problem*
Lacking Be without or deficient in	*I enjoy using a computer, it is only that I don't own one. So I have limited time to spend on it*
Moved Characterized by intense feeling	*I am getting more experienced in using the computer. I knew a little bit about computers when I came here, but since I started practicing using computers, I am gaining a lot. As a person who lives in a rural area I am now the same as the person who lives in an urban area. Thank you for your support*
Optimistic The belief that good will triumph and virtue will be rewarded	*It was difficult for me in the beginning but I managed to do the work that was allocated to me. Now I have gained computer skills; I'm computer literate!*
Pleased Feelings of pleasure and satisfaction	*They gave the opportunity and a good teacher who is flexible and effective*
Powerless Without ability, influence, or power	*I don't have access to computers at my working place, neither do my learners, so this makes me afraid to buy myself a computer*
Reproach Expressing disapproval or disappointment	*Because computers were for those who had money. In my school there were no computers. I did not have the privilege to even see what it is*

Code and Description	Quote
Ashamed Worthy of or causing shame or disgrace	*There were no computers at the time when I grew up*
Sharing Spontaneous sharing of information	*I want to improve; using a computer in my everyday life. My sister works in Saudi Arabia, so I want to communicate with her through e-mails on the computer*
Stimulated Excited and invigorated, anxious to put to practice	*I want to be better skilled. Computer study is a skill just like driving. If one does not drive for a long time, the skill will fade away or be easily forgotten. I also want to buy my own so that I can practice every day, and even do my unfinished tasks at home*
Successful Obtaining a favorable outcome	*Before coming to class, somebody did try to introduce us to computer literacy but he was not well informed, so it became confusing to understand, but now with this course, I can see the light and computer literacy is all about practice. There were no problems in passing the module*
Thankful Pleased and relieved	*Computer literacy training is a good course: It helped me a lot in using a computer. I benefited a lot and thanks to Potchefstroom for introducing this course*
Touched Affected or provoked	*Because North-West University has provided us with a kind lady. A teacher who did not shout at us but helped us; as I am the one who has no picture of how to use a computer*
Yearning A longing, almost wistful desire	*If I had access to using a computer I would be good and this will have helped in getting information to be used for personal and teaching purposes*
Conscious Competent Model	
Unconscious incompetent The person is not aware of the existence or relevance of the skill	*As from now, I am going to buy my own cellphone because now I know something about computers* *Because computers are everything in life and is helpful*
Conscious incompetent The person becomes aware of the existence and relevance of the skill	*The statements will make me improve my skills because I am blank* *If I can give myself time to study computers, I will be able to use it for every activity. I need someone to assist me*
Conscious competent The person achieves 'conscious competence' in a skill when they can perform it reliably at will	*The course went very well and I hope to improve and work harder from what I have learnt. I believe practice makes perfect* *I can now work on my own. I was afraid before being exposed to computers*
Unconscious competent The skill becomes so practiced that it enters the unconscious parts of the brain—it becomes 'second nature'	*In high school I studied computers from grade 8 to 12. I grew up with a computer in the house. Working on a computer was second nature to me*

Conclusions and Recommendations

The researchers developed the following *Model for Computer Literacy Learning* (Figure 3) from the cumulative results of this research (Table 2). The model consists of two continuums, namely (i) the Technophobia—Technophilia continuum, and (ii) the Incompetent—Competent continuum. Two continuums divide the model into four quadrants, (i) *incredible*, (ii) *absorbed*, (iii) *hopeless*, and (iv) *hopeful*.

The current investigation yielded a make-up of 2% of the total group of participants who were competent were also technophobic (*incredible*); 43% of the total group who were incompetent were also technophobic (*hopeless*); 20% of the total group who were competent were also technophiliac (*absorbed*); while 35% of the total group of participants who were incompetent were also technophiliac (*hopeful*). This model could be useful to other researchers who are interested in computer literacy learning emotions, not only as a theoretical model, but also as a conceptual research framework.

During the systematic investigation of developing a Social Transformational Learning Technology Implementation Framework to address the needs of the SCTE, the needs of the learners, faculty members, and the constraints of the organization all need to be considered. In compiling such a framework, the current study has identified themes that will assist in establishing relevance while extracting meaning from the lived experiences of research participants.

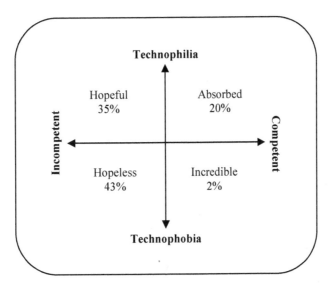

Figure 3: Model for Computer Literacy Learning Emotions

Pro-active interventions focus on initial assessment of computer literacy, followed by custom made ICT training for meaningful implementation of ODL to alleviate technophobia and promote engagement in utilizing computers and appropriate learning technologies. Consequential interventions could include introducing teacher students to learner management systems, online libraries, electronic information searching, applicable online study methods, as well as basic academic reading and writing competencies. Once an acceptable level of computer literacy has been established, technological acceptance should enable some online and other interactive media alternatives such as mobile learning. Progressive integration of technology into teaching and learning could develop together with e-readiness for the older generation of teacher students. Young teacher students may require less custom made intervention relating to digital literacy.

References

Abbad, M. M., Morris, D., & De Nahlik, C. (2009). Looking under the bonnet: factors affecting student adoption of e-learning systems in Jordan. *International Review of Research in Open and Distance Learning, 10*(2). Retrieved from http://www.irrodl.org/index.php/irrodl/article/view/596/1232

Agyei, D. D., & Voogt, J. M. (2011). Exploring the potential of the will, skills, tool model in Ghana: Predicting prospective and practicing teachers' use of technology. *Computers & Education, 56*(1), 91-100.

Anderson, A. A. (1996). Predictors of computer anxiety and performance in information systems. *Computers in Human Behavior, 12*(1), 61-77.

Anderson, T., Rourke, L., Garrison, D. R., & Archer, W. (2001). Assessing Teaching Presence in a Computer Conferencing Context. *Journal of Asynchronous Learning Networks, 5*(2), 1-17.

Buddhamind.com. (s.a.). A list of human emotions. Retrieved 8 December, 2011, from http://www.buddhamind.info/leftside/actives/drama/key-word.htm

Businessballs.com. (2010). Conscious competence learning model: stages of learning--unconscious incompetence to unconscious competence. Retrieved 9 December, 2011, from http://www.businessballs.com/consciouscompetencelearningmodel.htm

Chang, T. F. (2005, 5-8 July 2005). *Can emotional design change people's attitude on the web site?* Paper presented at the 5th IEEE International Conference on Advanced Learning Technologies (ICALT '05), Kaohsiung, Taiwan.

Chen, J., & Luo, Q. (2006). *Research on e-learning system model based on affective computing* Paper presented at the 7th International Conference on Computer-Aided Industrial Design and Conceptual Design, 2006

(CAIDCD '06) from http://www.mendeley.com/research/research-on-elearning-system-model-based-on-affective-computing/

Christensen, R., & Knezek, G. (2008). Self-report measures and findings for information technology attitudes and competencies. In J. Voogt & G. Knezek (Eds.), *International handbook of information technology in primary and secondary education* (pp. 349-365). New York: Springer.

Conti-Ramsden, G., Durkin, K., & Walker, A. J. (2010). Computer anxiety: A comparison of adolescents with and without a history of specific language impairment (SLI). *Computers & Education, 54*(1), 136-145.

Cramer, D., & Howitt, D. (2004). *The SAGE dictionary of statistics*. London: SAGE.

Dictionary.com. (2011). Emotion. Retrieved 30 June, 2011, from http://dictionary.reference.com/browse/emotion

Ellis, S., & Steyn, H. S. (2003). Practical significance (effect sizes) versus or in combination with statistical significance (p-values). *Management Dynamics, 12*(4), 51-53.

Goleman, D. (1995). *Emotional intelligence*. New York: Bantam Books.

Ingleton, C. (1999). *Emotion in learning: a neglected dynamic*. Paper presented at the HERDSA Annual International Conference. Retrieved 12 December 2011, from http://www.herdsa.org.au/wp-content/uploads/conference/1999/pdf/Ingleton.PDF

Jones, A. (2010). Affective issues in learning technologies: emotional responses to technology and technology's role in supporting socio-emotional skills. *Journal of Interactive Media in Education, 9*, 1-22. Retrieved from http://jime.open.ac.uk/article/2010-9

Jung, C. G. (1990). *The archetypes and the collective unconscious* (Vol. 10th, Part I, Bollingen Series XX). New York: Princeton University Press.

Kort, B., Reilly, R., & Picard, R. (2001, 6-8 August 2001). *Affective model of interplay between emotions and learning: reengineering educational pedagogy--building a Learning Companion*. Paper presented at the Advanced Learning Technologies, 2001, Madison, WI.

Krathwohl, D. R., Bloom, B. S., & Masia, B. B. (1973). *Taxonomy of Educational Objectives, the Classification of Educational Goals. Handbook II: Affective Domain*. New York: David Mckay Co., Inc.

Kruger, J., & Dunning, D. (1999). Unskilled and unaware of it: how difficulties in recognizing one's own incompetence lead to inflated self-assessments. *Journal of Personality and Social Psychology, 77*(6), 1121-1134.

Leech, N. L., & Onwuegbuzie, A. J. (2009). A typology of mixed methods research designs. *Qual Quant, 43*(2009), 265-275.

Merriam, S. B. (1998). *Qualitative Research and Case Study Application in Education*. San Francisco, CA: Jossey-Bass.

MIT Media Lab. (s.a.). Affective communication. Retrieved 29 April, 2011, from http://affect.media.mit.edu/areas.php?id=communication

Moolman, H. B., & Blignaut, A. S. (2008). Get set! e-ready, ... e-learn! The e-readiness of warehouse workers. *Educational Technology & Society, 11*(1), 168-182.

Papastergiou, M. (2010). Enhancing Physical Education and Sport Science students' self-efficacy and attitudes regarding Information and Communication Technologies through a computer literacy course. *Computers & Education, 54*(1), 298-308.

Psychpage.com. (2010). Resources for students and professionals. Retrieved 8 December, 2011, from http://www.psychpage.com/learning/library/assess/feelings.html

Saldăna, J. (2009). *The coding manual for qualitative researchers*. London: Sage.

South Africa. (2004). White paper on e-Education. Retrieved 9 December, 2011, from http://www.info.gov.za/view/DownloadFileAction?id=68767

Verhoeven, J. C., Heerwegh, D., & De Wit, K. (2010). Information and communication technologies in the life of university freshmen: An analysis of change. *Computers & Education, 55*(1), 53-66.

Walter Hottinga.com. (2011). Feelings--a list of describing words. Retrieved 5 June, 2011, from http://www.walterhottinga.com/personal-development/feelings-a-list-of-describing-words/

7 Looking for evidence of change: Evaluation in the Teaching Teachers for the Future project

Peter R. Albion

Introduction

In late 2007 Australia elected a Government that included in its platform an initiative dubbed the Digital Education Revolution (DER), which was intended to achieve a national vision for Information and Communication Technology (ICT) in schools (DEEWR, 2008). That vision, for students to graduate with relevant knowledge and skills for using ICT and for learning to be improved by integration of ICT, had been articulated at the beginning of the century but had been mostly left to the states and territories to implement separately. The DER represented a commitment to implementing the vision at a national level and one of its most visible elements was funding to increase the provision of computers in schools to a ratio of 1:1 for years 9 to 12 by 2011.

Although the initial and most widely visible thrust of the DER was provision of equipment, the implementation roadmap recognized that "educators require the pedagogical knowledge, confidence, skills, resources and support to creatively and effectively use online tools and systems to engage students" (AICTEC, 2009, p. 6). That document referred to providing "professional learning opportunities for existing teachers to upgrade or develop proficiency in the effective and innovative/creative educational use of ICT" and ensuring "that the national graduate teacher standards include rigorous requirements regarding the use of technology in teaching" (AICTEC, 2009, p. 8). In 2010 funding was made available through an ICT Innovation Fund for projects to improve the capabilities of pre-service and in-service teachers for working with ICT and to build the capacity of school leaders to support ICT integration (DEEWR, 2010).

Teaching Teachers for the Future (TTF) was the successful bid for the ICT Innovation Fund element targeted to pre-service teacher education. A group acting on behalf of the Australian Council of Deans of Education led the bid and its implementation involves all thirty-nine Australian higher education institutions that prepare teachers. TTF comprises three components, namely, extension of the graduate teacher standards being developed by the Australian Institute for Teaching and School Leadership (aitsl.edu.au) to include ICT dimensions, development of professional learning packages demonstrating how ICT can be integrated in the first four subjects of the new Australian curriculum (ttf.edu.au), and development of a National Support Network (NSN) to drive systemic change in the treatment of ICT in teacher education. The third component provided funding to each of the participating institutions to employ for one year the equivalent of an additional person with experience in classroom integration of ICT and to release a senior academic half-time to manage the project within each institution. Discussions during the development of the TTF proposal identified Technological Pedagogical Content Knowledge (TPACK) (Mishra & Koehler, 2006; Thompson & Mishra, 2007) as a useful framework for talking about the development of pre-service teachers' capabilities for working with ICT. TPACK was adopted as the underlying framework for the TTF project and is informing the development of packages in the second component and the work of the NSN.

The TTF proposal included a commitment to evaluation of each of the three components. For the first component, the extension to the national professional standards for graduate teachers, the commitment was to a trial of the dimensions and associated evidence guides in teacher education programs participating in the third component, followed by refinement of the dimensions for eventual wider application. For the second component, the exemplar packages, an independent evaluator was appointed and the evaluation was to include trial of the packages in participating programs and collection of data from participants through questionnaires and interviews.

Given that the central goal of the TTF project is to build the ICT in Education (ICTE) proficiency of graduate teachers and that the majority of the funding and effort toward that goal has been committed in the third component, the focus of evaluation for the third component was to be changes in the ICTE capabilities of pre-service teachers. Because the TPACK framework has informed the TTF project to the extent that the project documents speak of developing TPACK capacity, it was natural for the evaluation to focus on changes in TPACK. To plan and manage the evaluation of the third component across thirty-nine institutions, a

Research and Evaluation Working Group (REWG) was established with representation from multiple participating sites and additional members with relevant expertise drawn from the Australian Association for Research in Education (AARE).

Measurement of TPACK

The TTF project involves 39 institutions that enroll several thousand pre-service teachers in teacher preparation programs. Obtaining comparable measures of TPACK on that scale presents significant logistical challenges and ideally would be done using a method that is known to be valid and reliable. A method suitable for online administration to large numbers of respondents would be a convenient solution for the TTF project with its requirement to collect data from several thousand pre-service teachers at sites around Australia.

In a review of methods and instruments for measuring TPACK, Abbitt (2011) reported that he located 33 studies that included an assessment of TPACK and that 20 of those had been conducted in the context of pre-service teacher programs. Another review reported identifying 141 instruments that measured some aspect of TPACK (Koehler, Shin, & Mishra, 2011). Despite this apparent plethora of instruments for measuring TPACK or some aspects of it, there appears to be no widely accepted instrument that has emerged as the obvious choice.

Attempts to measure TPACK date from the earliest writing on the framework. Koehler and Mishra (2005) asked 17 participants about their perceptions the TPACK model elements during a design course. The analysis showed that participants increased their thinking about all seven TPACK elements during the course. A subsequent study with 24 participants (Koehler, Mishra, & Yahya, 2007) using a similar design traced development of TPACK elements, confirming the development of stronger interconnections among the initially separate topics of technology, content and pedagogy over time. These studies demonstrated the development of TPACK over time but did not provide a methodology for measurement of TPACK with larger groups.

Despite the apparent enthusiasm for TPACK as a framework for thinking about teachers' work with ICT, Graham (2011) has argued that there is still considerable variation in the understanding of TPACK and its component elements. In his view the published research on TPACK has weaknesses in relation to criteria for theory building that suggest a need for increased effort by researchers to build common definitions. One of the key issues identified by Graham relates to whether the areas of intersection in the TPACK framework diagram should be understood as integrative or transformative. He notes that, although the diagram suggests an integrative model in which elements such as Technological Pedagogical Knowledge (TPK) represent a combination or mixture of Technological Knowledge (TK) and Pedagogical Knowledge (PK), the language used by Mishra and Koehler (2006) implies a transformative understanding in which TPK is a distinct form of knowledge that is not merely the sum of its parts. In the absence of agreement among researchers on this and other aspects of the theory it is difficult to imagine how it could be possible to construct a satisfactory method of measurement for TPACK.

Lack of common understanding of the TPACK constructs among researchers may have contributed to the emergence of variations in the models used as the basis for development of instruments in some studies. Angeli and Valanides (2009) proposed ICT-TPCK as a strand within TPCK and used a combination of peer, expert, and self-assessment demonstrated in two design tasks guided by a list of criteria to assess the TPCK of 215 pre-service elementary teachers in 3 separate semester cohorts. They reported that students' total ICT-TPCK increased from the first task to the second. The similarities between ICT-TPCK and the general TPACK framework are sufficient that the criteria used in this study could be adapted for wider use but the method of task-based assessment of individuals would not be scalable to a project such as TTF. Lee and Tsai (2010) proposed TPCK-W as a variation of the TPACK framework in which the World Wide Web was the focal technology. Although this study may have lessons about the process of constructing an instrument to measure TPACK, its narrowed focus on Web technology makes it unsuitable for application in the TTF project.

Even when the TPACK framework is used in its generic form without variations such as those described above (Angeli & Valanides, 2009; Lee & Tsai, 2010), there is liable to be some degree of specificity around the content being learned or the technology being deployed. These factors present challenges for development of instruments that are both general enough to be useful in different contexts and specific enough to avoid vague generalities. A 24 item questionnaire was developed for use with K-12 online educators using processes including review by an expert panel and a think-aloud pilot to ensure construct validity and consistent interpretation of items (Archambault & Crippen, 2009). Analysis of data from 596 respondents indicated that the instrument was valid and reliable but the items are specific to online education and not suitable for wider use without modification.

Graham, Cox, and Velasquez (2009) considered self-report and performance-based assessment of artifacts as methods for measuring TPACK development in pre-service teachers. They noted that performance assessment is time consuming and unsuitable for use with large groups or when a quick result is required and that questionnaires suffer from difficulties in framing questions to address the TPACK constructs and inconsistent interpretation by respondents. They developed a questionnaire to measure TPACK constructs but reported that items did not load as expected in factor analysis. Another study using a questionnaire to measure TPACK confidence of science teachers (Graham, Burgoyne, et al., 2009) addressed only the four technology-related elements (TPCK, TPK, TCK, and TK) of the TPACK framework with the content-related items linked to science. They reported significant increases in each element from start to finish of an intensive professional development program but the small number of participants did not permit tests for construct validity of the instrument.

A community of researchers interested in the TPACK framework is developing and the TPACK website (www.tpck.org) provides one focal point for activity including approaches to the measurement of TPACK. An instrument available from that website comprises items developed from the framework and subjected to construct validity checks by an expert panel before being administered to 87 elementary pre-service teachers (Schmidt, et al., 2009). The scales attributed to the various elements of the TPACK framework returned Alpha reliability values that ranged from 0.75 to 0.92, suggesting that the instrument is reliable and could be used confidently where the elementary subjects represented in the content scales are appropriate.

Although it would be desirable to have a direct measure of teachers' TPACK, performance-based measures are not practicable for large numbers and self-report measures are also problematic (Graham, Cox, et al., 2009). There is good evidence that teachers' behaviors with ICT are strongly influenced by their related levels of confidence (Ertmer & Ottenbreit-Leftwich, 2010). Hence there would be value in the development and use of self-report instruments to measure teachers' confidence to perform TPACK-related behaviors in the expectation that higher levels of such confidence would be related to increased performance of the behaviors. The *TPACK Confidence Survey (TCS)* was developed to audit the TPACK confidence of final year pre-service teachers at two Australian universities (Albion, Jamieson-Proctor, & Finger, 2010). The 20 items used to measure TPACK confidence had been developed and validated in a previous study of ICT integration in schools in which teachers had been asked to indicate how often students in their classes used ICT for a variety of learning tasks (Jamieson-Proctor, Watson, Finger, Grimbeek, & Burnett, 2007). For the *TCS* the items were modified to ask pre-service teachers to indicate their level of confidence for facilitating such use by students in their classes, thereby indicating their levels of confidence for performing TPACK-related behaviors (Albion, et al., 2010).

TTF Project Evaluation Plan

The leaders of the TTF project were aware of the prior work with the *TCS* (Albion, et al., 2010) and recruited the authors, who were already involved with the project in their own institutions, to the REWG with the intention of using the TCS as the basis of an instrument to measure change in TPACK-related capabilities. The REWG had one face-to-face meeting but otherwise worked by teleconference and email from January to April 2011 to develop the necessary instruments and protocols. It included members experienced in Rasch and other forms of analysis who conducted some analysis of items used in the *TCS* study and made a strong case for ensuring that any instrument would include items likely to attract a range of responses from students. Hence the REWG began by developing a varied collection of about 100 potential items with a focus on the elements of the TPACK framework that included technology (TK, TPK, TCK, and TPCK). Through discussion and successive rounds of editing this collection was reduced so that the core of the final questionnaire comprised 56 items classified as TPK (24), TCK (8), and TPCK (24, including 20 items carried over from the *TCS*). When complete the questionnaire also included parallel scales using the same items to assess pre-service teachers' perceptions of the future usefulness of the TPACK-related behaviors. Table 1 displays sample items developed for each of the sections with the relevant stems for the confidence scales.

For the TPK items the usefulness stem was "How useful do you consider it will be for you, as a teacher, to be able to use ICT to …". Equivalent changes were made to construct the usefulness scales for the other sets of items. Both sets of items were presented using 7-point scales with anchors at 0 (Not confident, Not useful), 3 (Moderately confident, Moderately useful), and 6 (Extremely confident, Extremely useful) with an additional non-scoring alternative labeled as "Unable to judge". In addition to the confidence and usefulness scales described above, the final questionnaire included a range of demographic items and an additional 9 items related to the extensions to the graduate standards being developed in the first component of TTF.

Technological Pedagogical Knowledge (TPK)

How confident are you that you have the knowledge, skills and abilities to use ICT to …

  Demonstrate knowledge of the range of ICT to engage students

  Access, record, manage, and analyze student assessment data

Technological Content Knowledge (TCK)

How confident are you that you have the knowledge, skills and abilities to …

  Design learning sequences, lesson plans and assessment that use ICT to develop students' Mathematics knowledge, attitudes and skills

  Implement meaningful use of ICT by students in achieving Mathematics curriculum goals

ICT integration - TPCK

How confident are you that you have the knowledge, skills and abilities to support students' use of ICT to …

  Demonstrate what they have learned

  Integrate different media to create appropriate products

Table 1: Sample items from the core groups in the instrument

The TTF project was approved for funding from the beginning of 2011 until mid-2012 but complications in the project arrangements delayed the release of funding until April 2011. As a consequence the work of the project did not begin in most institutions until April 2011, thereby delaying the date at which pre-test data could be collected. Because the funding conditions required final reports to be submitted in June 2012 it was thought impractical to attempt to collect and analyze post-test data in 2012, leaving late 2011 as the only time available for administration of the post-test questionnaire. The effect of a TTF intervention on pre-service teachers was expected to be limited by the combination of a late start to the project and its interventions, the short time between pre-test and post-test, and the variations in programs among institutions that would affect what, if any, intervention could occur between pre-test and post-test. These factors and commitment to seeking alternative forms of evidence led the REWG to consider additional approaches to evaluation. The Most Significant Change (MSC) technique (Dart & Davies, 2003) was adopted as a suitable methodology for collecting a wider range of data about any possible effects of the TTF project on teacher preparation programs.

Data Collection and Analysis

The questionnaire was presented online using Qualtrics (www.qualtrics.com) software, which supported tailoring of demographic questions according to enrolment so that respondents saw only the choices about campus, program and course that applied to their institution. Once the questionnaire was ready in late April 2011, coordinators at each of the participating institutions arranged to issue email invitations to all students enrolled in their teacher preparation programs. The administration schedule varied by institution because of factors including assessment periods, delays in obtaining ethical clearance, and students being absent on professional experience. The period of availability of the questionnaire was ultimately extended to July to accommodate these differences. In total 10433 complete or partially complete responses were collected.

Analysis of the national data set is being undertaken by a team with experience in analysis of complex datasets and will include comparison among groups of participants, including institutions, which can be distinguished according to responses to demographic and other items in the questionnaire. Participating institutions have been provided with summaries of responses for the national set and for their own institutions and with the individual responses for their own institution. The results presented in this paper are based on the national summary and the data provided for one Queensland regional university. They represent preliminary analyses and may be subject to adjustment following completion of the analyses being conducted nationally.

Table 2 presents results from the national dataset and for the one university. Means have been calculated for confidence and usefulness on the groups of items originally identified as representing TPACK elements. This analysis has been conducted on the raw data prior to the national analysis confirming (or not) the structure of the instrument. The means obtained for the regional university were significantly higher than the national means (Z-test, $p < 0.01$) for five of the six measures. Inspection of the results for individual items in the scales revealed that the means for the regional university were higher than the national means on all item and significantly higher (Z-test, $p < 0.01$) for 39 of the 56 items and 32 of the 56 items on the confidence and usefulness scales respectively.

	Item group	National			University					
		N	Mean	SD	N	Mean	SD	Z	p	
Confidence										
	TPK	9422	4.01	1.40	508	4.24	1.34	3.72	<.001	*
	TCK	6304	3.81	1.45	390	4.01	1.38	2.70	.003	*
	TPCK	8816	3.99	1.38	486	4.13	1.32	2.41	.008	*
Usefulness										
	TPK	9416	5.15	1.11	508	5.29	1.00	3.04	.001	*
	TCK	6218	5.26	1.06	390	5.32	1.02	1.07	.142	
	TPCK	8809	5.11	1.11	485	5.23	1.02	2.45	.007	*

Table 2: Mean scores on subscales for national and university datasets (* = significant at 1%)

The regional university in this study had participated in previous studies (Albion, et al., 2010) that included 20 items from the *TCS* subsequently incorporated in the TPCK subscale of the TTF instrument. Hence there was the possibility of examining trends in responses to those items by comparing results from the 2009 and 2010 questionnaires with the 2011 dataset. Table 3 presents results from those 20 common items for the 2011 datasets from the national pool and the regional university together with values for Z and estimates of the probability. Although, as shown in Table 2, the university mean on the TPCK subscale is significantly higher than the national mean ($Z = 2.41$, $p = .008$), the means on just 9 of the 20 items are significantly higher ($p < 0.01$).

	How confident are you that you have the knowledge, skills and abilities to support students' use of ICT to ...	National (N = 8816)		University (N = 486)				
		M	SD	M	SD	Z	p	
1	provide motivation for curriculum tasks	4.12	1.32	4.23	1.25	1.98	.024	
2	develop functional competencies in a specified curriculum area	3.82	1.35	3.99	1.31	2.84	.002	*
3	actively construct knowledge that integrates curriculum areas	3.93	1.35	4.07	1.32	2.31	.011	
4	actively construct their own knowledge in collaboration with their peers and others	3.99	1.34	4.07	1.28	1.36	.087	
5	synthesise their knowledge	3.80	1.39	3.93	1.32	2.14	.016	
6	demonstrate what they have learned	4.18	1.34	4.31	1.28	2.22	.013	
7	acquire the knowledge, skills, abilities and attitudes to deal with on-going technological change	4.09	1.41	4.24	1.35	2.29	.011	
8	integrate different media to create appropriate products	3.87	1.43	4.00	1.38	2.04	.021	
9	develop deep understanding about a topic of interest relevant to the curriculum area/s being studied	4.07	1.32	4.17	1.30	1.70	.045	
10	support elements of the learning process	4.05	1.32	4.20	1.27	2.57	.005	*
11	develop understanding of the world	4.23	1.31	4.36	1.22	2.28	.011	
12	plan and/or manage curriculum projects	4.03	1.37	4.20	1.32	2.74	.003	*
13	engage in sustained involvement with curriculum activities	3.98	1.36	4.17	1.33	3.04	.001	*

	How confident are you that you have the knowledge, skills and abilities to support students' use of ICT to ...	National (N = 8816		University (N = 486)				
		M	SD	M	SD	Z	p	
14	undertake formative and/or summative assessment	3.97	1.42	4.16	1.37	2.87	.002	*
15	engage in independent learning through access to education at a time, place and pace of their own choosing	4.06	1.41	4.26	1.36	3.06	.001	*
16	gain intercultural understanding	3.87	1.37	4.03	1.32	2.42	.008	*
17	acquire awareness of the global implications of ICT-based technologies on society	3.81	1.40	3.93	1.34	1.84	.033	
18	communicate with others locally and globally	4.34	1.38	4.50	1.27	2.62	.004	*
19	understand and participate in the changing knowledge economy	3.79	1.45	4.05	1.35	4.09	<.001	*
20	critically evaluate their own and society's values	3.90	1.39	4.01	1.33	1.68	.046	

Table 3: National and regional university 2011 results for selected TPCK subscale items (* = significant at 1%)

The questionnaire administered in 2009 and 2010 used a 4-point scale scored from 1 to 4 with anchors of 'No confidence', 'Some confidence', 'Confident', and 'Very confident'. That was different from the 7-point scale described above for use in the 2011 questionnaire. Hence comparison of trend data first required conversion of data to comparable scales. Table 4 presents the 4-point and 7-point scales aligned to show how the 2011 data were converted to the 4-point scale by recoding with half-points inserted. Alternative conversions using the anchor points to establish linkages were considered but discarded because they appeared to inflate the converted scores making the differences appear larger than for the conversion shown in Table 4 which was preferred as more conservative.

2011 National scale	Not confident			Moderately confident			Extremely confident
	0	1	2	3	4	5	6
2009-10 University scale	1	1.5	2	2.5	3	3.5	4
	No confidence		Some confidence		Confident		Very confident

Table 4: Conversion of 7-point scale to 4-point scale for comparison

Table 5 presents comparative results for the 20 common questions included in the TPACK confidence instruments administered in 2009, 2010 and 2011. Average scores for the 20 items in each of the questionnaires are also included at the foot of the table and Z scores and P values are included for the 2009-2010 and 2010-2011 comparisons. There were no significant differences found between scores recorded in 2009 and those recorded in 2010. In contrast, using the conversion from 7-point to 4-point scale shown in Table 4, the mean scores for all items were significantly higher (p < 0.01) in 2011 than in 2010.

	How confident are you that you have the knowledge, skills and abilities to support students' use of ICT to ...	2009 (N = 136)		2010 (N = 450)				2011 (N = 486)				
		M	SD	M	SD	Z	P	M	SD	Z	P	
1	provide motivation for curriculum tasks	2.94	.70	2.93	.73	-.15	.885	3.11	.62	2.80	.003	*
2	develop functional competencies in a specified curriculum area	2.76	.75	2.76	.75	<.01	.999	3.00	.66	3.34	<.001	*
3	actively construct knowledge that integrates curriculum areas	2.86	.74	2.79	.76	-.96	.338	3.03	.66	3.46	<.001	*
4	actively construct their own knowledge in collaboration with their peers and others	2.88	.69	2.86	.75	-.29	.774	3.04	.64	2.65	.004	*
5	synthesise their knowledge	2.86	.73	2.78	.74	-	.265	2.96	.66	2.65	.004	*

	How confident are you that you have the knowledge, skills and abilities to support students' use of ICT to ...	2009 (N = 136)		2010 (N = 450)				2011 (N = 486)				
		M	SD	M	SD	Z	P	M	SD	Z	P	
6	demonstrate what they have learned	3.04	.66	2.94	.74	1.11 -1.50	.134	3.15	.64	3.34	<.001	*
7	acquire the knowledge, skills, abilities and attitudes to deal with on-going technological change	2.72	.77	2.76	.79	.52	.600	3.12	.67	4.90	<.001	*
8	integrate different media to create appropriate products	2.63	.87	2.71	.83	.94	.346	3.00	.69	3.58	<.001	*
9	develop deep understanding about a topic of interest relevant to the curriculum area/s being studied	2.90	.76	2.86	.75	-.54	.589	3.09	.65	3.15	.001	*
10	support elements of the learning process	2.93	.69	2.90	.72	-.44	.660	3.10	.63	3.06	.001	*
11	develop understanding of the world	2.75	.75	2.74	.78	-.13	.893	3.18	.61	6.25	<.001	*
12	plan and/or manage curriculum projects	2.88	.72	2.82	.76	-.84	.402	3.10	.66	4.08	<.001	*
13	engage in sustained involvement with curriculum activities	2.81	.74	2.79	.76	-.27	.784	3.08	.66	4.18	<.001	*
14	undertake formative and/or summative assessment	2.96	.71	2.91	.8	-.70	.486	3.08	.69	2.45	.007	*
15	engage in independent learning through access to education at a time, place and pace of their own choosing	2.87	.76	2.82	.75	-.68	.498	3.13	.68	4.29	<.001	*
16	gain intercultural understanding	2.81	.77	2.81	.76	<.01	.999	3.01	.66	2.78	.003	*
17	acquire awareness of the global implications of ICT-based technologies on society	2.60	.82	2.61	.80	.13	.900	2.97	.67	4.63	<.001	*
18	communicate with others locally and globally	3.09	.73	3.02	.74	-.97	.332	3.25	.64	3.31	<.001	*
19	understand and participate in the changing knowledge economy	2.66	.76	2.66	.79	<.01	.999	3.03	.67	5.05	<.001	*
20	critically evaluate their own and society's values	2.75	.74	2.76	.77	.14	.892	3.01	.67	3.46	<.001	*
	Mean score	2.84	.74	2.81	.76	-.32	.749	3.07	.66	3.69	<.001	*

Table 5: Trends in regional university scores for common TPCK items across 2009-2011 (* = significant at 1%)

Respondents to the 2009 questionnaire were all students in the final year of their teacher education programs but respondents in 2010 and 2011 included students at all stages in their programs. Those datasets were analyzed using ANOVA with the TPCK subscale score as the dependent variable and responses grouped by stage in the program. Because the questions about progress in the program were asked differently in 2010 and 2011, the groups were not directly comparable but it was possible to identify students according to relative time from completing their program. There were significant differences ($p < .05$) found between groups for both the 2010, [$F_{(3, 425)} = 8.44$, $p < .000$], and 2011, [$F_{(5, 498)} = 2.246$, $p = .049$], respondents. Post hoc tests revealed that respondents in the final year of their program reported the highest mean scores.

Discussion

As described above, preliminary analysis of data from the national questionnaire suggests that, for students in the regional university, the mean self-rated confidence for performing TPACK-related behaviors is significantly higher than the national average for their peers in other teacher preparation institutions. That preliminary finding is subject to confirmation when the results of the national analyses of the data are available. The national analysis will establish the characteristics of the instrument used for data collection and will include cross-institutional and other comparisons that will explore any significant differences between identifiable groups within the national sample. In the meantime there is value for the regional university in considering what significance the differences revealed in the questionnaire data may have for the teacher preparation program and its development.

Of the six subscales reported in Table 2, respondents from the regional university reported significantly higher means on five, including all three for confidence related to various elements of TPACK. The implication is that, compared to students in other teacher preparation programs, students at the regional university feel better prepared for working with ICT in their future classrooms. This is a positive outcome for the teacher preparation programs at the regional university and, to the extent that teachers' confidence levels influence their use of ICT in their, it is an indicator of potential for enhanced use of ICT in those classrooms.

The significantly higher means on the 20 items of the TPCK confidence subscale found for respondents in the final year of their teacher preparation program confirm that confidence increases during the program of study. Although it is possible that some of the increase might be related to maturation or other factors unrelated to the teacher preparation program, it seems likely that much of the increase is attributable to experiences within the program, which includes both a specific course on *ICT and Pedagogy* and a variety of other experiences of ICT used for learning embedded in other courses.

The apparent increase in means on the 20 common items across the 2009 to 2011 period also bears examination. The results presented in Table 5 are for final year students in 2009 and students across all years in 2010 and 2011. Those results show no significant increase from 2009 to 2010 but significant increases on all items from 2010 to 2011. When the data for final year students only are examined there are 6 items with significant ($p < .01$) increases from 2009 to 2010 and 2 with significant increases from 2010 to 2011. However, all 20 items exhibit significant differences ($p < .01$) from 2009 to 2011. The implication is that the mean TPCK confidence of students in the program has been increasing from year to year.

On the basis of this preliminary analysis it appears that the teacher preparation program at the regional university is making a difference to graduates' TPACK confidence as manifested in higher mean scores for final year students, that the extent of that difference has increased over the past three years, and that on average graduates from this university report higher levels of confidence than the average of graduates nationally.

In considering potential explanations for these differences, two factors emerge. One is the reintroduction from 2010 of the *ICT and Pedagogy* course, which is taken by most students in the third year of their fourth year program. Final year students responding to the 2011 questionnaire will have completed that course. A second factor is the offering of all courses entirely online, as well as on the three campuses, from 2009. Although only about 50% of students in any course are studying online, the online offering has affected the way that courses are developed such that all students in the courses are likely to interact with at least parts of the online materials. In doing so they experience learning with ICT in ways that they might not have done in conventionally offered courses and that experience is likely to affect their knowledge of learning and teaching with ICT and their confidence for working with ICT. Those effects may be evident in their increased scores on the TPACK confidence scales.

As noted above, the apparent affirmation of the success of teacher preparation at the regional university in building TPACK confidence awaits confirmation through the analysis being undertaken by the national team. If it does emerge that this university, and others, are more successful at inculcating TPACK confidence as measured by the instrument then identifying practices that contribute to that success may contribute substantially to meeting the TTF project goals. The short time available for interventions supported by the project reduces the likelihood of identifying valuable practices through differences between pre-test and post-test scores. However, if it may be possible to identify such practices through cross-institutional comparisons and for them to be adopted more widely in appropriate contexts.

References

Abbitt, J. T. (2011). Measuring Technological Pedagogical Content Knowledge in Preservice Teacher Education: A Review of Current Methods and Instruments. *Journal of Research on Technology in Education, 43*(4), 281-300.

AICTEC. (2009). Digital Education Revolution Implementation Roadmap Retrieved October 17, 2010, from http://www.deewr.gov.au/Schooling/DigitalEducationRevolution/Documents/AICTEC_DER_ROADMAPAdvice.pdf

Albion, P. R., Jamieson-Proctor, R., & Finger, G. (2010). Auditing the TPACK Confidence of Australian Pre-Service Teachers: The TPACK Confidence Survey (TCS). In C. Maddux, D. Gibson & B. Dodge (Eds.), *Research Highlights in Technology and Teacher Education 2010* (pp. 303-312). Chesapeake, VA: Society for Information Technology in Teacher Education.

Angeli, C., & Valanides, N. (2009). Epistemological and methodological issues for the conceptualization, development, and assessment of ICT-TPCK: Advances in technological pedagogical content knowledge (TPCK). *Computers & Education, 52*(1), 154-168.

Archambault, L., & Crippen, K. (2009). Examining TPACK Among K-12 Online Distance Educators in the United States. *Contemporary Issues in Technology and Teacher Education, 9*(1), 71-88. Retrieved from http://www.citejournal.org/vol9/iss1/general/article2.cfm

Dart, J., & Davies, R. (2003). A Dialogical, Story-Based Evaluation Tool: The Most Significant Change Technique. *American Journal of Evaluation, 24*(2), 137-155. doi: 10.1177/109821400302400202

DEEWR. (2008). Success through partnership: Achieving a national vision for ICT in schools Retrieved October 17, 2010, from http://www.deewr.gov.au/Schooling/DigitalEducationRevolution/Documents/DERStrategicPlan.pdf

DEEWR. (2010). ICT Innovation Fund Guidelines 2010 - 2012 Retrieved October 17, 2010, from http://www.deewr.gov.au/Schooling/DigitalEducationRevolution/DigitalStrategyforTeachers/Documents/ICTInnovationGuidelines.pdf

Ertmer, P. A., & Ottenbreit-Leftwich, A. T. (2010). Teacher Technology Change: How Knowledge, Confidence, Beliefs, and Culture Intersect. *Journal of Research on Technology in Education, 42*(3), 255-284.

Graham, C., Cox, S., & Velasquez, A. (2009). *Teaching and Measuring TPACK Development in Two Preservice Teacher Preparation Programs.* Paper presented at the Society for Information Technology and Teacher Education International Conference 2009, Charleston, SC, USA.

Graham, C. R. (2011). Theoretical considerations for understanding technological pedagogical content knowledge (TPACK). *Computers & Education, 57*(3), 1953-1960. doi: 10.1016/j.compedu.2011.04.010

Graham, C. R., Burgoyne, N., Cantrell, P., Smith, L., St. Clair, L., & Harris, R. (2009). Measuring the TPACK Confidence of Inservice Science Teachers. *Techtrends, 53*(5), 70-79.

Jamieson-Proctor, R., Watson, G., Finger, G., Grimbeek, P., & Burnett, P. C. (2007). Measuring the Use of Information and Communication Technologies (ICTs) in the Classroom. *Computers in the Schools, 24*(1), 167 - 184.

Koehler, M. J., & Mishra, P. (2005). What happens when teachers design educational technology? The development of technological pedagogical content knowledge. *Journal of Educational Computing Research, 32*(2), 131-152.

Koehler, M. J., Mishra, P., & Yahya, K. (2007). Tracing the development of teacher knowledge in a design seminar: Integrating content, pedagogy and technology. *Computers & Education, 49*(3), 740-762.

Koehler, M. J., Shin, T. S., & Mishra, P. (2011). How Do We Measure TPACK? Let Me Count the Ways. In R. N. Ronau, C. R. Rakes & M. L. Niess (Eds.), *Educational Technology, Teacher Knowledge, and Classroom Impact: A Research Handbook on Frameworks and Approaches* (pp. 16-31). Hershey, PA: Information Science Reference.

Lee, M.-H., & Tsai, C.-C. (2010). Exploring teachers' perceived self efficacy and technological pedagogical content knowledge with respect to educational use of the World Wide Web. *Instructional Science, 38*(1), 1-21. doi: 10.1007/s11251-008-9075-4

Mishra, P., & Koehler, M. J. (2006). Technological Pedagogical Content Knowledge: A Framework for Teacher Knowledge. *Teachers College Record, 108*, 1017-1054.

Schmidt, D., Baran, E., Thompson, A., Koehler, M., Punya, M., & Shin, T. (2009). *Examining Preservice Teachers' Development of Technological Pedagogical Content Knowledge in an Introductory Instructional Technology Course.* Paper presented at the Society for Information Technology and Teacher Education International Conference 2009, Charleston, SC, USA.

Thompson, A. D., & Mishra, P. (2007). Breaking News: TPCK becomes TPACK! *Journal of Computing in Teacher Education, 24*(2), 38,64.

PART 3 SOCIAL MEDIA OPPORTUNITIES

8 Impact of Using Facebook as a Social Learning Platform to Connect High School Students with Working Adults

Yuhei Yamauchi, Toru Fujimoto, Kaoru Takahashi Junko Araki Yusuke Otsuji Hisashi Suzuki

Introduction

The recent rapid diffusion of social media such as Twitter and Facebook have enabled users to connect with people more than ever before. In addition, students are using social media at school for various purposes such as communicating, sharing personal experiences, and exchanging information with others (Selwyn 2009 & Hew 2011). While educators are concerned with how they should treat such media in order to prevent classroom disruption, social media also provides affordable resources that can build a social learning environment in a way that was not possible before. Recent research shows that the educational use of social media has significant potential as a learning management system (Yu et al. 2010, Lampe 2011, Junco 2012).

While most research on the educational use of social media has been conducted primarily on college students, we considered that high school students might also gain great merit by utilizing social media for the following reasons. First, high school students, especially those in Japan, do not have frequent opportunities to connect with people beyond their own generation other than their parents and teachers. In addition, high school students currently have a lack of resources and opportunities to consider their future plans. Although the competitive culture excessively influences the need to get accepted into prestigious colleges, high schools are not necessarily offering adequate resources for students, especially in regard to making wise decisions about their future. As a result, high school students in Japan unfortunately lack information that would equip them to answer questions such as what kind of institutions are universities and corporations, why should I go to college, why should I go out into society, and if I should go there, what is likely to happen? While it is true that students have to face and answer these types of questions on their own, students might be able to find a better future plan by utilizing social media as a support system, which can lead them to a more prosperous future not only for themselves but also for the universities that they enter and for society in general.

Our project team at the Benesse Department of Educational Advanced Technology (BEAT) at the University of Tokyo has been researching on the educational use of social media since 2010. Our previous study (Yamauchi et al. 2011) conducted a project-based social learning program called the "Socla" program, which connected high school students with working adults through Twitter. The participants consisted of 17 high school students who worked on individual study projects that focused on their future plans on the basis of their specific interests. During the program, they worked on the project at home and communicated with other students and adult supporters via Twitter. On the final day of the program, each student reported the outcomes of their work in face-to-face presentations. The students' responses from a questionnaire indicated that their interaction with other participants made the program enjoyable. Such positive responses also indicated the potential of using Twitter as a successful learning platform.

Based on the outcomes of the first-year program, we have made the following changes to the overall structure of the program. First, the system platform for the program was changed from Twitter to Facebook owing to the following reasons: (a) while Twitter is easy to use and it enhances casual communication, postings disappear quickly, which makes it difficult to reflect upon afterwards; (b) Twitter does not have adequate functions to create a sense of space for an online study group; and (c) to address the privacy concerns of parents and teachers, we required more flexibility regarding privacy control settings so that the students could work safely in a social networking environment. Facebook offers easy-to-use online communication tools with a safe environment in terms of privacy. In addition, it offers group page functions that can be used for closed groups as well as for public ones. Second, facilitators were included to support the students in addition to volunteer supporters. The facilitators guided the students and encouraged the supporters to help the students at crucial points during the program. Because such roles are difficult to expect from volunteer supporters, some type of leadership role was required for the success of the overall program.

After applying these changes, we conducted the second-year "Socla" program in summer 2011. The purpose of this study was to investigate the impact of using Facebook as a learning management system for high school students in individual learning projects. We especially focused on how the students and adult volunteer supporters interacted with one another and what the students gained from the program in terms of their views on the future. The remainder of the paper describes the details of the study and the results.

The Study

Participants

We conducted the Socla program for a two-week period from July 30 to August 13, 2011. The participants included 23 second-year high school students (six from the Great East Japan Earthquake disaster area that were separately recruited, and 17 from the general application), 32 volunteer supporters publicly recruited from Facebook (including 22 working adults, seven undergraduate students, and three graduate students), and six facilitators consisting of graduate students majoring in education or education-related fields.

Program Overview

The program was created as a blended-project learning approach by combining on-site, face-to-face guidance, and follow-up sessions with online project learning through Facebook. Before the program began, the students were asked to choose a study theme category for their project (academic plan, career plan, and life plan) on the basis of their individual interests. The students were prearranged into six small study groups (consisting of three to four students, five to six supporters, and one facilitator for each group).

On the first day of the program, the students participated in a face-to-face orientation session held at the University of Tokyo. The students formulated questions and a hypothesis for their individual projects and planned a study schedule. In addition, they attended a hands-on introductory lecture on how to safely use Facebook. The project themes that the students worked on are shown in (Tab. 1).

Theme Category	Study Theme
Academic Plan (College Life)	What can you gain from participating in a study abroad program while attending a college of medical science?
	What is a seminar in a college like?
	What kind of options are there after graduation for female students pursuing a career in the sciences?
Career Plan (Career and Job Search)	Can female students majoring in the arts and social sciences become an airline pilot?
	Is it useful to go to college when pursuing a career as a stage or voice actor?
	What career should you pursue to solve global poverty issues (Ministry of Foreign Affairs, United Nations, or Non-Government Organizations)?
Life Plan (Marriage and Everyday Life)	Is it difficult for philosophy majors to find jobs?
	What skills should I acquire to become an information study teacher?
	Relationship between married life and pursuing personal goals.

Table 1: Examples of Study Project Themes Chosen by Students.

After the guidance session, the students worked on individual study projects through Facebook for a period of two weeks. In addition, they searched the Internet for relevant resources and answers to their research questions, while the facilitators and volunteer supporters encouraged them and responded to their inquiries. During the project, the students were required to submit (a) a daily report to share their progress with others; (b) an interim report that outlined their final report; and (c) a final report that summarized their findings and conclusions. All these reports were submitted on the program's Facebook group message board and shared with peer students and the supporters. The participants were encouraged to press the "like" button and comment on the reports throughout the program. The students were also suggested to submit public questions through both the program's Facebook page and Twitter. In this case, the facilitators and supporters assisted them to form adequate questions that could gain the expected responses that they required.

For example, a student from a private high school in the Tokyo Prefecture worked on his project theme of "What can you gain from participating in a study abroad program while attending a college of medical science?" Through surveys conducted on Facebook, he discovered that there were both advantages and disadvantages of studying abroad while attending a college of medical science. In addition, he noticed that studying abroad as a student offered few merits in furthering one's career because it generally lacked actual participation in medical activities. In addition, he concluded that timing and a clear vision of the future were some of the most important factors when choosing a suitable study abroad program. Another student from a public high school in the Miyagi Prefecture worked on his theme of "Is it difficult for philosophy majors to find jobs?" Based on the advice from the volunteer supporters, he conducted research on the careers of graduates in philosophy and in which fields the skills and knowledge acquired could be used. It was also suggested that he conduct interviews with specific alumni in the philosophy field as well as a professor in the department of philosophy. After his research, he concluded that philosophy is about realizing inconsistencies in everyday life. While deep critical thinking is what companies seek in its newly hired employees, finding a job can still be difficult regardless of the study field. Therefore, the only way forward is to continue making the "right" type of decisions and putting efforts in the right direction.

All these activities were conducted on the Facebook group pages, which were set up for use by small study groups. The participants were also permitted and welcomed to use the open forum for both casual conversation and information sharing. In addition, a group page was created so that the facilitators and volunteer supporters could communicate with one another outside the students' circles. On the final day of the program, the students presented their project outcomes in a poster session format. The supporters and facilitators attended the session and offered feedback and other helpful comments. All students completed the program requirements, although one student could not attend the poster session (owing to personal reasons) and submitted the required presentation materials via Facebook.

Data Collection

We collected pre- and post-survey data to explore how the program was accepted by the students and how their experience in the program affected their individual views on the future. At the beginning and end of the program, the students were asked to answer the following questionnaires in terms of their overall impression of the use of Facebook, their experience in the program, and their views on learning about their individual future paths. Moreover, we collected all postings from the group pages and analyzed how the students communicated with one another during the program.

Findings and Discussions

Students' Impression of the Use of Facebook

Using a five-point Likert scale (1: totally non-applicable to 5: totally applicable), the students answered 14 questions regarding their views on the use of Facebook and their overall experiences in the program. According to the responses, most students found that Facebook was easy to use, and they enjoyed communicating with others through the application. Regarding their impression of the program in general, they found the program to be both enjoyable and engaging (Fig. 1).

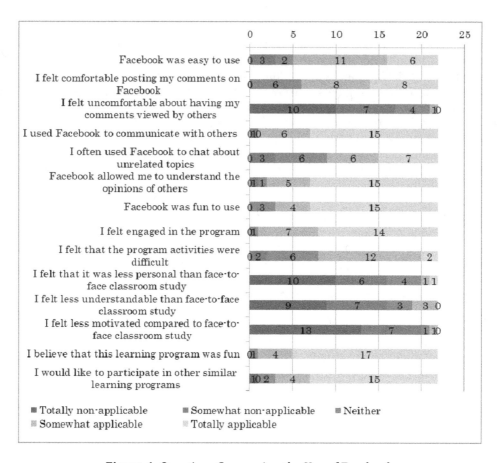

Figure 1: Questions Concerning the Use of Facebook

Students' Views on Learning and their Future

Using a five-point Likert scale (1: totally non-applicable to 5: totally applicable), the students answered questions about their overall views on learning. The comparison of results from pre- and post-survey data indicated that more students believed that it was useful to receive advice from their superiors (Pre<Post P = .031), and information found on the Internet was useful toward their study (Pre<Post P = .018, Tab. 2).

	Mean		Std.	
	Pre	Post	Pre	Post
Q1–9. Usefulness of advice from superiors	4.26	4.74	.730	.619
Q1–10 Usefulness of information from the Internet	3.57	4.04	.945	.638

Table 2: Students' Views on Learning

Regarding their views on the future, the results revealed that the students changed their views about future and career decisions once the program was completed. In addition, the students generally felt more hopeful about their future (Pre<Post P = .005, Tab. 3).

	Mean		Std.	
	Pre	Post	Pre	Post
Q2–6 Feeling hopeful toward the future	3.26	3.7	1.054	.926

Table 3: Students' Hopes for the Future

The relationship between the students' views on feeling hopeful toward the future and their impression of Facebook and the program indicated that the students who enjoyed the program and the use of the application generally felt more hopeful toward their own future (Tab. 4).

	Q4–4 Interchanged on Facebook	Q4–6 Gained opinions on Facebook	Q4–7 Enjoyed Facebook	Q4–8 Participated well	Q4–10 Felt personal	Q4–11 Understandable program	Q4–12 Engaging program
Q2-5 Hope for future	.475 *	.59 **	.456 *	.579 *	–.484 *	–.447 *	–.687 **
*p < .05, **p < .01 N = 23 (except Q4–6: N = 22)							

Table 4: Relationship between Students' Hopes for the Future and Impression of the use of Facebook and the Program

In addition, it was identified that more students felt less anxious about choosing a career path (Pre<Post P = .026) and that they considered seeking advice about career choices. Finally, it was also identified that more students believed that external factors did in fact influence career paths (Pre<Post P = .024).

Students' Impression of Facilitators and Supporters

The facilitators and supporters provided useful information and advice for the students throughout the entire program. The results of the survey showed that most students found them helpful toward their study (Fig. 2).

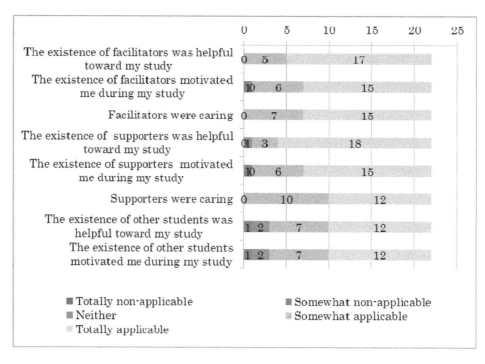

Figure 2: Questions Concerning Relationship in the Program Community

Posting-Log Analysis

During the program, a total of 5,108 messages were posted on the Socla program's Facebook group page. 786 messages were new threads that initiated communication, and 4,322 posts were responses to them. The high school students posted approximately 60% of the posts whereas the rest were from the facilitators and supporters. A unique feature of Facebook allows viewers to indicate whether they liked the post by pressing the "like" button. In this case, 3,676 "likes" were counted for the 5,108 posts. The diagram of social network analysis visualized that the social network connected with the "like" button included more network paths among the participants than that connected with comment responses (Fig. 3). Even the supporters who did not frequently participate in the program had multiple connections. The participants commented that the "like" button was a convenient feature that expressed their acknowledgement of and interest in the postings of others. It could be inferred that the use of this button allowed the participants to easily react to postings, which then further enhanced social interaction within the community.

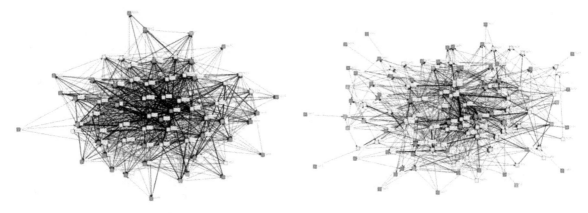

Figure 3: Network Diagram of Participants' Connection with the "Like" Button (left) versus with Comment Responses (right)

Other Technical Issues

During the program period, we did not face serious technical issues. However, subtle technical matters caused problems for some participants. First, at the outset of the program, Facebook had some technical issues in terms of compatibility among the different web browsers and operation systems. For example, the group document function did not work properly on Microsoft's Internet Explorer browser. In some cases, postings would disappear, which frustrated students who wrote long documents (without backups) because they had to rewrite them all over again. For the participants using Mac OS computers, postings on the Facebook group wall disappeared as well. Because these issues occurred inconsistently, it took some time to detect and troubleshoot these problems. In addition, occasional updates of Facebook functions and user interfaces were another cause of technical issues. Because Facebook made changes to their system settings during the program period, we had to adjust to the system changes by updating instructional materials and announcing these changes to the participants. Although these specific technical problems were eventually resolved, immediate technical troubleshooting was performed to reduce unnecessary frustration caused by these unexpected issues.

Second, the privacy policy we assumed for the program conflicted with some technical operations. As noted, the students were requested to set their privacy settings to a "friends only" status during the program, especially in regard to the safety of novice Facebook users. This privacy policy helped us manage the program in a safer manner, and it addressed the concern of both parents and teachers regarding the online privacy protection of their children and students, respectively. However, a technical issue occurred regarding information sharing while using the "note" function. Because the students and supporters were not necessarily connected with one another as Facebook "friends", some supporters could not browse other students' notes on their personal pages. Although Facebook offers flexibility in regard to the control of privacy settings for every user, novice users cannot use such flexibility owing to its complexity. Therefore, we advised the participants to use the group page to share their work progress instead of using the "note" function on their private pages.

Conclusions

In summary, the project successfully offered an engaging opportunity that enhanced social interactions between students and adult supporters in the process of learning. The result of the survey revealed that students gained a positive attitude about their future paths through the program. In addition, it was indicated that their experiences from the program alleviated some level of anxiety in regard to choosing future paths. The group function offered by Facebook was used to establish a semiopen and safe learning platform for high school students who were not necessarily accustomed to participating in a social networking community. Some technical issues were recognized during the program, and these problems need to be addressed to gain the most from this type of program in the future.

Moreover, the study illustrated that the continuous support from the facilitators and supporters largely contributed toward engaging the students in their individual projects. Research has shown that encouraging students to actively participate in online communication can be a difficult task and such students become frustrated without immediate feedback (Aoki & Molnar 2011). Even when comment responses become difficult to process, participants can interact using the "like" button. This type of system function eases the overall burden of responders and contributes toward a positive and active social learning community. Although the e-tutor's role is still a pivotal factor toward engagement in collaborative learning, system functions help reduce the tutors' load by providing immediate feedback to the students.

Finally, because this program was conducted with a relatively small number of students, future research should be performed on a larger population, possibly on an international scale. To expand the scale of the program, it is necessary to accept participants without requiring face-to-face sessions. We will continue to improve the program and establish it as a model of a social learning program that offers students the opportunity to connect and work with adults in a safe and engaging environment.

References

Aoki, K., & Molnar, P. (2011). Project-Based International Collaborative Learning using Web 2.0 Tools for Authentic Learning of Foreign Language and 21st Century Skills. In T. Bastiaens & M. Ebner (Eds.), *Proceedings of World Conference on Educational Multimedia, Hypermedia and Telecommunications, 2011,* Chesapeake, VA: AACE. 2349-2353. Retrieved from http://www.editlib.org/p/38186.

Bingham, T., & Conner, M. (2010). *The New Social Learning - A Guide to Transforming Organizations Through Social Media,* Berret-Koehler Publishers.

Hew, K. (2011). Students' and teachers' use of Facebook. *Computers in Human Behavior, 27,* 662-676.

Junco, R. (2012). The relationship between frequency of Facebook use, participation in Facebook activities, and student engagement. *Computers & Education,* 58(1), 162-171.

Lambropoulos, N., Faulkner, X., & Culwin, F. (2011). Supporting social awareness in collaborative e-learning. *British Journal of Educational Technology,* 43(2), 295-306.

Lampe, C., Wohn, D. Y., Vitak, J., Ellison, N., & Wash, R. (2011). Student use of Facebook for organizing collaborative classroom activities. *International Journal of Computer-Supported Collaborative Learning,* 6, 329-347.

Selwyn, N. (2009). Faceworking: exploring students' education-related use of Facebook. *Learning, Media and Technology,* 34(2), 157-174.

Yamauchi, Y., Tsubakimoto, M., Kitamura, S., Misono, T., Otsuji, Y., & Suzuki, H. (2011). The Socla Project: an Attempt to Build an Innovative Study Environment through SNS Linkage of Second-Year High School Students and Working Adults. In T. Bastiaens & M. Ebner (Eds.), *Proceedings of World Conference on Educational Multimedia, Hypermedia and Telecommunications, 2011,* Chesapeake, VA: AACE. 1276-1282

Yu, A.Y., Tian, S.W., Vogel, D., & Kwok, R.C. (2010). Can learning be virtually boosted? An investigation of online social networking impacts, *Computers & Education,* 55(4), 1494-1503.

Wang, Q., Woo, H. L., Quek, C. L., Yang, Y., & Liu, M. (2011). Using the Facebook group as a learning management system: An exploratory study. *British Journal of Educational Technology,* 43(3), 428-438.

9 Social Networking Services in E-Learning

Peter Weber, Hannes Rothe

1. Introduction

The Community of Inquiry Framework (CoI) with its collaborative-constructivist perspective on learning presents a holistic perspective on the process of creating and delivering e-learning experiences (Garrison, 2011). It focuses on the opportunities of technology enabled learning but is at the same time based on the premise "that a community of learners is an essential, core element of an educational experience when higher-order learning is the desired learning outcome" (Garrison, 2011, p. 19). E-learning is considered as a means of facilitating interactivity and creating a quality learning experience, as it is in the Net Economy class, which will be discussed with regard to the use of a social networking service in this paper.

The CoI-framework identifies three interdependent elements as the constituent parts of successful (e-) learning experiences: (1) social presence, (2) cognitive presence, and (3) teaching presence. Social presence is defined as "the ability of participants to identify with a group, communicate purposefully in a trusting environment, and develop personal and affective relationships progressively by way of projecting their individual personalities" (Garrison, 2011, p. 23). Cognitive presence in contrast is understood as "the extent to which learners are able to construct and confirm meaning through sustained reflection and discourse in a critical community of inquiry" (Garrison, Anderson, & Archer, 2001, p. 11). Finally, teaching presence is "the design, facilitation and direction of cognitive and social processes for the purpose of realizing personally meaningful and educationally worthwhile learning outcomes" (Anderson, Rourke, Garrison, & Archer, 2001). It is this teaching presence that combines and balances the elements of a community of inquiry in the overall setting to guarantee worthwhile e-learning.

In this paper we will focus on the possible role that social networking services (SNSs) can play with regard to the need for social presence. In order to make them a supporter of social presence, teaching presence is necessary, since the use of the SNS during the learning experience needs to be designed and steered carefully. As corresponding elements of teaching presence, we developed a phase concept and a team building approach that are both meant to guarantee an intensive and meaningful use of the SNS in our course.

The practical background of our study is a class named Net Economy, which we offered as a cross-location Virtual Collaborative Learning (VCL) setting in 2011 and in which we implemented NING as an easy-to-use social networking service. This implementation of a SNS derived from a rich background of conference discussions during the last few years (Gabriel, Gersch, Weber, Le, & Lehr, 2009; Gersch, Lehr, & Weber, 2011). In this paper we will describe and discuss our social networking approach with regard to the following guiding questions:

1) How did the students use and value the SNS as the central coordination platform for the Net Economy class?
2) Did the phase concept and the team building approach verifiably influence the use of the SNS in a positive way?

To do so, in Chapter 2 we introduce the Net Economy class with its phase concept and team building approach. In Chapter 3, we review literature on social networks and social networking services in educational settings and describe our approach of implementing NING in the Net Economy class. In Chapter 4, we outline a set of hypotheses with regard to the above guiding questions, which we will then analyze and discuss with the help of data from the Net Economy class. The paper closes with a brief conclusion and outlook in Chapter 5.

2. The Net Economy Class

In the framework of an international learning network we have been offering cross-location e-learning courses entitled "Net Economy" for more than four years. The setting targets participants with heterogeneous educational backgrounds in the fields of business and economics, business informatics, and educational sciences, and with different cultural backgrounds from Germany (Bochum, Berlin, Dresden, Soest), Turkey (Istanbul), China (Shanghai), Lithuania (Kaunas), Latvia (Riga), and Indonesia (Jakarta). It aims at virtual collaborative learning.

Every Net Economy class is divided into the three phases 'preparation phase, production phase' and 'case study phase.' Throughout the course, project work is conducted in small teams of 4-6 students and across locations, both in terms of team composition as well as presentation and discussion of findings through video conferencing. By separating these phases, learning and working processes are structured as a project with the use of predefined milestones. The students are asked to present and discuss their findings at steering committees and within phase-specific final presentations. These steering committees and final presentations are held at each location and are merged together through video conferencing.

During the preparation phase the teams are set up and the students can acquire the information and skills (e.g., media skills) necessary to accomplish the tasks during the production and case study phases. Whereas in the prior Net Economy classes the teams were established by the course instructors, in our new approach the task of defining the teams was delegated to the students during the preparation phase. The students had to create a personal profile on a class specific social networking site, which then served as their application to become a team member. The questions concerning the profile prompted a critical reflection of their individual strengths, weaknesses and previous experiences relating to both the topics of the class and virtual collaboration (e.g., use of media). Based on the profiles that the students developed, the instructors appointed the team leaders who then recruited their teammates. The composition of the teams was thereby restricted with regard to group size and the number of team members from each participating location: A maximum of six students per team and a maximum of two students per location and per team were allowed. Shortly prior to the start of the production phase, conflicts were resolved by the instructors, if necessary. By delegating the task of group definition we intended to strengthen the students' self-reliance and their identification with their teams – thus social presence.

During the second phase of the setting (production phase) the participants experience a "learning through teaching approach" (Biswas, Leelawong, Schwartz, & Vye, 2005). Under their instructors' guidance they develop multimedia learning materials, such as web-based training systems or Google sites on methods of strategic management or current IT-topics. This way they gain new scholarly insights and prepare themselves for the final case study phase.

The case study phase as the third part of the learning scenario provides the students with a case study, for example on electronic marketplaces (2008/2009), grocery home delivery (2010/2011), or the use of Web 2.0 applications within and between companies (2011/2012). While working on these case studies, the students can apply their newly acquired knowledge to concrete business challenges. The second and third phases are thus linked together in a way that the learning material created in the production phase provides a substantive knowledge base for the tasks within this case study phase. In addition, all three phases are meant to provide opportunities for the participants to foster international contacts and to gain experience in cross-cultural technology-based learning and work.

Figure 2 summarizes the learning scenario Net Economy with regard to its global context, the use of information and communication technology (especially Web 2.0 applications), its three phases, the student teams, and its blended learning character.

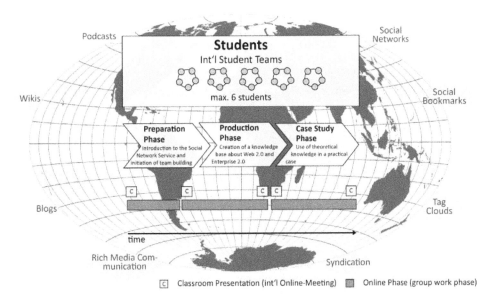

Figure 1: **The Net Economy Learning Scenario**

In summary, the Net Economy class is not only associated with cognitive but also affective and psychomotor learning goals. These learning goals relate to content, use of media, e-learning, cooperative working and learning as well as the presentation of work results. In addition to the impartment of new knowledge, attention is paid to fostering and deepening vocational abilities such as virtual collaboration, use of Web 2.0 applications, and life-long learning (Safran, Helic, & Gütl, 2007).

3. Social Networking Services in E-Learning and as Part of the Net Economy Setting

During the last few years, the terms and concepts of "social networks, social networking services, social networking sites" and "social media" gained a strong position in e-learning research (Liccardi et al., 2007; Liu, Kalk, Kinney, & Orr, 2012). While all these terms refer to some sort of social context, they still address different things and need to be differentiated. According to Liccardi et al. (2007), social networks are "a social structure of nodes that represent individuals (or organizations) and the relationships between them within a certain domain" (Liccardi et al., 2007, p. 225). Social networks are thus technologically neutral and have existed long before the rise of today's famous Web 2.0 social networks, like Facebook, LinkedIn, etc. These in contrast are examples of social networking sites or social networking services, websites referred to as SNSs, which are used to build online networks (Boyd & Ellison, 2007; Dalsgaard, 2008). SNS allow for the creation of personal profiles and relationships with friends, in order to share activities, media (photos, documents, links, etc.) and thoughts. They foster interaction and help people stay up-to-date regarding news and activities within their network of friends and support them in enhancing their network (Boyd & Ellison, 2007; Garrison, 2011). SNSs are one occurrence of the Web 2.0 with its many well-known applications (like blogs and wikis) and its characteristic fundamental shift regarding the role of web users as participants in content creation (O'Reilly, 2005).

As with other Web 2.0 applications, because of the great success and widespread popularity of SNSs like Facebook, educators are exploring the possibilities and challenges of using them for educational purposes (Liu et al., 2012). Many researchers contend that the integration of SNSs into teaching and learning is expected by the students (as the 'net generation' Oblinger & Oblinger, 2005), both as a means of teaching and learning and as a subject matter with regard to the workplace of the future (Hamat, Embi, & Hassan, 2012). Others emphasize the opportunities deriving from the SNS-functionality, such as interactivity and collaboration, which allow for the co-construction of knowledge as pursued in collaborative-constructivist approaches (Hamat et al., 2012). Also, SNSs are advocated as indirect support of educational settings, in which they can serve as 'social glue' and help the students persist and be more successful by making them feel well connected and part of a community (Garrison, 2011; Hamat et al., 2012).

On the other hand, skeptics point out that SNSs are far from being successfully established as a means of education and e-learning. Roblyer et al. (2010) for example argue that students understand SNSs as social and not as educational and that this makes a big difference (Roblyer, McDaniel, Webb, Herman, & Witty, 2010). Garrison (2011) points at the high degree of spontaneity and superficiality usually connected to SNS usage, which contradicts the educational paradigm (Garrison, 2011). Thus, despite the promising arguments mentioned above, the question whether students and instructors will adopt SNSs and whether their use will be educationally worthwhile remains crucial and needs explicit consideration (Garrison, 2011; Hartshorne & Ajjan, 2009).

When evaluating these arguments with regard to a potential use of SNSs in an educational setting, the many different options and objectives for implementing SNS need to be considered. While some authors discuss the use of public SNS, like Facebook, for direct or indirect instructional purposes (Mendoza, 2009; O'Donoghue & Warman, 2009; Roblyer et al., 2010), others intend to facilitate the features of SNS through a dedicated and closed social networking site or within established learning management systems (Colazzo, Magagnino, Molinari, & Villa, 2008; Gersch et al., 2011).

In our case, we chose NING to create a dedicated SNS for the Net Economy course, in order to connect the students from the participating locations and help them feel being part of the community in the e-learning setting. We intended to provide the 'social glue' for the group of participants as a whole and for the teams in particular. The students should see and feel the cross-location and international character of the class at any time and we wanted them to feel motivated to use the SNS also for social exchange with the other students. NING allowed us to create a custom social network with typical features like profile pages, relationships, latest activity streams, status updates, photos, videos, blogs, groups, forums, announcements, etc. (www.ning.com). Using the NING Plus membership, we also gained access to real-time analytics providing additional transparency. For example, we could gather insights on how the SNS was used during the course, what relationships were established by the students, and who were the most and the least active members. In addition, we integrated the SNSs with Google services, so that students were able to log on with their Google accounts, which they needed for developing documents and websites collaboratively. In summary, the SNS served as the main coordination instrument and was the starting point for all activities related to the class. It also provided us instructors with comprehensive data on the social activities of the participants.

In the following Chapter we will provide and analyze data on SNS usage during the Net Economy class to discuss the guiding questions from Chapter 1. By answering these questions, we intend to support others who consider whether to use SNSs in e-learning by providing an example of SNS-implementation and by delivering first evidence for the controllability of the adoption of SNS through teaching presence measures.

4. Hypothesis and Empirical Study

Our efforts of developing a SNS-concept for the Net Economy class with the described phase concept and team-building approach as means of teaching presence were based on the following hypothesis:

1) How will the students use and value the SNS as the central coordination platform for the class?

H1a)   *The SNS will be used continuously and intensely throughout the complete course.*
        Since the SNS was established as the one and only official coordination platform for the class and since it was intended to serve as the major instrument for students to project themselves and to correspond with each other, we expected a constant and significant use in all phases of the setting.

H1b)   *The SNS usage will reach a level that indicates a purely social application in addition to the activities related to the tasks of the class.*
        Due to of the cross-location and international background of the class and because of the students' high familiarity with SNS usage for private purposes, we expected them to use the functionalities of the SNS, like friendships, photo and video sharing, 'I Like' ratings, etc. also outside the course setting, thus leading to a higher network density. By promoting this we wanted them to feel being part of the community.

2) Will the phase concept and the team building approach verifiably influence the use of the SNS in a positive way?

H2a)   *The self-responsible team building approach as part of the preparation phase will lead to a higher degree of connection building during preparation phase compared to the production phase or case study phase.*

Among other reasons, we developed the team building approach in order to facilitate an intensive use of the SNS. By turning the students' profiles into their applications for team membership, we intended to put the SNS of the class on a firm footing right from the beginning.

H2b)   *The team building approach with its emphasis on the role of the team managers will make the team managers central agents of the SNS as a whole.*

By choosing only the team managers and making them responsible for the acquisition of the other team members, we intended to position central hubs within the network who at the same time feel responsible for the activities of their groups. We therefore expected the centrality of the team managers – on average – to be higher than the centrality of the other students.

Data

The dataset collected in this research was obtained from the described Net Economy course 2011/2012. The overall sample consists of 166 students who joined the class specific SNS, which we developed using NING. Fifty-two of these students came from an Indonesian university, while the other 114 students came from four German universities. All network specific data was gathered with the help of a javascript, written to analyze user profiles automatically for interconnections between students. A meaningful interconnection was assumed and counted every time students formed a virtual 'friendship'. Additional information about the usage of the SNS was obtained from GoogleAnalytics as a client-side web analysis tool.

Methodology and Variables

Our first hypothesis (H1a) will be tested using visiting data for the SNS during all three phases of the class. The other hypotheses deal with interconnection-data of the students. We test H1b by interpreting summarized data about the use of certain SNS-features (e.g., photo sharing) and students' relationships with each other as indicators of a social use of the SNS. To derive whether the described team building approach lead to a significant amount of connections during the preparation phase (H2a), we will present connection building data on a time scale. Finally, we compare the team manager role with students who were not primarily responsible for the team building process by using discriminant analysis (H2b). Therefore, we defined the following dependent, independent and control variables for illustrative purposes and for the discriminant analysis:

Dependent Variable

For our first hypothesis UNIQUE_VISITORS of the SNS as well as TIME_SPENT_ON_PAGE were measured by GoogleAnalytics data. All RELATIONS between the students as considered in the following hypotheses were gathered by counting the friendships between students as active relationships. This seems reasonable since students had to form friendships in the forefront of further virtual interaction on the SNS. In any event, no additional means of measuring the intensity and quality of interactions between students were included at this point. As a result, the overall connections could only be aggregated nominally, leading to an unweighted and undirected representation of the network. Finally, TEAMLEADERS are operationalized by a nominally coded dummy variable, which classifies students according to their role during the class.

Independent Variables

Based on the interconnections between students, CLOSENESS_CENTRALITY was measured and normalized to an interval of [0;1]. CLOSENESS_CENTRALITY describes the mean distance between a student and every other student in the network based on the shortest possible path between each pair (Borgatti & Everett, 2006; Freeman, 1979). Centrality thus rises with an increasing amount of direct friendships between a student and the other students on the SNS.

<u>Control Variables</u>

Since for all participating students the Net Economy course was part of a broader class schedule, possible interference with other classes needs to be considered. For example, it turned out that students from one university had exams during the semester, drawing their attention for a certain time period. Therefore, we control on UNIVERSITIES as dummy variables for each participating institution. Regression will thereby consist of only four instead of five dummies (we had five participating universities), since the number of universities is constrained and a fifth institution will be derived from non-classification to one of the other four universities.

The LOCAL_CLUSTERING_COEFFICIENT serves as a second control variable. It estimates the amount of possible interconnections between the direct neighbors of one node in the network and relates them to the actual sum of connections (Boccaletti, Latora, Moreno, Chavez, & Hwang, 2006, p. 183; Watts & Strogatz, 1998, p. 441). The coefficient thus reflects the extent of friends who are also befriended.

Results

H1a)   The SNS will be used continuously and intensely throughout the complete course.

Our first point of interest has been, whether the SNS was used intensely and continuously throughout all phases of the class. Figure 2 summarizes data gathered through GoogleAnalytics. Participation in terms of numbers of UNIQUE_VISITORS and TIME_SPENT_ON_PAGE has been highest during the last week of the

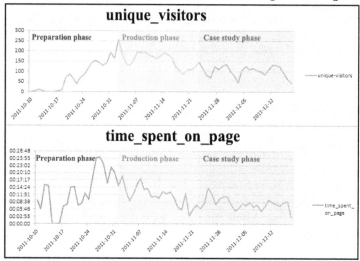

Figure 2: **Usage of SNS during phases of virtual class room setting**

preparation phase with 129 to 255 unique visitors per day who spent an average of approximately 20 minutes on the SNS. Thereby, every log-in from a different location or device is considered a UNIQUE_VISITOR, so that the 255 visitors also include students who logged-in more than once a day from different places or with different devices. Over the whole course, an average of 109 unique visitors spent 10:34 minutes per day on the SNS. From these findings, we can derive the fact that not every one of the 166 students logged onto the page daily.

During the preparation phase, the students created their individual profiles, browsed the profiles of their colleagues to get to know each other, and the team managers started setting up their teams. A peak in usage could thus be expected. There are two simple possible explanations for the lower overall averages of UNIQUE_VISITORS and TIME_SPENT_ON_PAGE in the subsequent phases of the class: One is that some students showed specific dedication and kept logging on to the SNS (possibly several times) every day, while others interacted on a less regular basis after the end of the preparation phase. The other explanation would be that (almost) all students reduced their SNS activity after the preparation phase and logged on to the SNS only every two or three days. In any case, since the SNS mainly offered communication tools like comments, blogs, discussion boards and instant messaging, the average 10 minutes must have been primarily spent on communication and interaction with other students. In addition, also the gradually declining average of

UNIQUE_VISITORS can be interpreted as an argument for the approval of hypothesis H1a, in which we assumed an intense and continuous use of the SNS throughout all three phases of the setting.

H1b)   The SNS usage will reach a level that indicates a purely social application besides the activities related to the tasks of the class.

The engagement of the students led to a total of 381 pictures which were shared through the SNS. In addition, 37 virtual discussion groups were formed voluntarily to debate team internals and the tasks of the class. Every student was engaged in an average of 11.78 friendships, with 0 friendships of one student indicating a drop out and 86 friendships marking the highest value. Since each team only consisted of six to seven members these numbers show that students formed far more relationships than implied by the instructional setting. This argument in favor of H1b is supported by the GoogleAnalytics data summarized in Figure 2. Especially during the production and case study phase, there was hardly any need to use the SNS for class specific reasons on a daily basis. In these phases, the students instead had to use GoogleServices to develop GoogleDocs and GoogleSites collaboratively. In conclusion, there are strong indicators for a purely social use of the SNSs, as assumed in H1b.

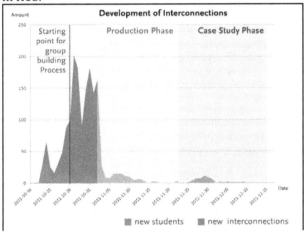

Figure 3: **Development of interconnection during phases of virtual classroom setting**

H2a)   The self-responsible team building approach as part of the preparation phase will lead to a higher degree of connection building during preparation phase compared to the production phase or case study phase.

Data for testing H2a is illustrated in Figure 3. Due to the team building approach described above, every student entered the SNS during the preparation phase. Consequently, 87.4% of all relationships between students were established during the preparation phase. Of the overall relationships, 64.74% therefore occurred after the nomination of the team managers. This nomination marked the beginning of the self-regulated team-building process. One possible explanation for the slowing down of the connection building activities would be a declining number of not yet established relationships. This means that if in the course of the setting almost all possible connections would have been established, network-density, defined as $L/(N(N-1)/2)$ with L representing the actual number of relationships and N the overall network size, would have tended to 1 (Scott, 1988, p. 114). Since the SNS in fact developed a density of 0.113, many additional relationships between students could have been added, so that this explanation has to be refused. The approval of H1a invalidates a significant decline of the SNS usage in general as a second possible explanation for the reduction in connection building. Thus, there are strong indicators for approval of H2a, in which we assumed that the development of the SNS usage in terms of interconnections was controlled by the self-regulated team building approach as part of the phase concept.

H2b)   The team building approach with its emphasis on the role of the team managers will make the team managers central agents of the SNS as a whole.

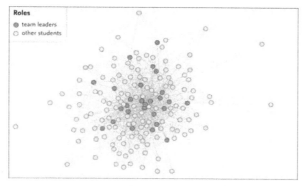

Figure 4: Distribution of team leaders in the overall network

Finally, we examined the relationship between the assignment of some students as team managers and their interconnection building activities. We therefore conducted a discriminant analysis to compare the team managers with the other students, who were not given primary responsibility for team creation. In total, 27 teams were built with each of them containing one team manager and five to six regular members from at least two different universities. The distribution of the team managers within the overall network is presented in Figure 4, which was created by using the network analysis software Gephi (Bastian, Heymann, & Jacomy). The arrangement of the nodes within the illustrated network has been accomplished via the Yifan Hu multilevel algorithm (Hu, 2005).

Although the illustration shows many team managers in the center of the network, we need to prove that our model is able to discriminate between team managers and all regular students by declining a null hypothesis by inferential statistics. The results of the according wilks' lambda test are presented in Table 1 (Decker, Rašković, & Brunsiek, 2010). As can be seen, our model significantly discriminates between team managers and other students. To depict which factors influenced discrimination most, Table 2 shows discrimination results in a structure matrix. The absolute characteristic of each factor indicates its specific influence on the proposed model. Only discriminators with a characteristic of more than +/- 0.4 can be interpreted as substantial (Carmines & Zeller, 1979, p. 60). Accordingly, no university influenced the discrimination substantially, which allows us to conclude that none of the universities were over-represented.

Our results show that only the proposed factors of network position (closeness_centrality) and local structure (local_clustering_coefficient) turned out to be substantial discriminators. The high influence of CLOSENESS_CENTRALITY thereby confirms H2b, in which team managers were assumed to be central hubs within the overall network. The strong negative influence of the LOCAL_CLUSTERING_COEFFICIENT in contrast shows that team leaders are locally less clustered than other students. To explain these occasions we need to look at the type of self-regulated team building process we carried out.

Test of Function(s)	Wilks' Lambda	Chi-square	df	Sig.
1	.815	32.293	6	.000

Table 4: Wilks' Lambda

Teamleader		Predicted Group Membership		
		0	1	Total
Count	0	104	32	136
	1	4	23	27
%	0	76.5	23.5	100.0
	1	14.8	85.2	100.0

Notes: 77.9% of original grouped cases correctly classified.

Table 2: **Classification Results**

	Function 1
closeness_centrality	.728
local_clustering_coefficient	-.727
university4	-.195
university3	.169
university2	.108
university1	.019

Notes: Pooled within-groups correlations between discriminating variables and standardized canonical discriminant functions.
Variables ordered by absolute size of correlation within function.

Table 3: **Structure Matrix**

During the preparation phase all team managers were asked to search for new team members and invite them into their group. As a result, some team managers formed a number of friendships with fellow students, with which they did not intensely collaborate afterwards. Local clustering between these 'neighbors' is conclusively lower.

Robustness of the discriminant analysis results could be assessed by matching proposed classification by discriminant model with actual groups. Table 3 presents the results of classification using a-priori-probability of 0.5 and depicts that 77.9% of the students were grouped correctly. Since there may be other factors which discriminate between the groups of (non-)team leaders, we find these results acceptable.

5. Conclusion

This paper exemplified and discussed the implementation of a SNS as the major coordination platform for an international cross-location e-learning setting. Due to the outstanding success of public SNS like Facebook and LinkedIn, SNSs are gaining growing attention also as educational means. By using a SNS, instead of a traditional learning management system, we intended to facilitate social presence, which can be considered a major factor of worthwhile e-learning experiences. We used NING as a course specific SNS which was mainly meant to emphasize the international character of the class and to support the 166 participating students from the 5 participating universities to feel being part of a valuable community. Social presence in general and thus also the described implementation of the SNS as part of our e-learning setting in particular need teaching presence in the sense of a careful design and control, in order to make an impact. We therefore established a phase concept and a team building approach, which both aimed at a successful adoption of the SNS by the students. With regard to these objectives of strong social presence due to the SNS and successful adoption of the SNS due the phase concept and team building approach, we discussed the following four hypotheses:

H1a)   *The SNS will be used continuously and intensely throughout the complete course.*

H1b)   *The SNS usage will reach a level that indicates a purely social application in addition to the activities related to the tasks of the class.*

H2a)   *The self-responsible team building approach as part of the preparation phase will lead to a higher degree of connection building during preparation phase compared to the production phase or case study phase.*

H2b)   *The team building approach with its emphasis on the role of the team managers will make the team managers central agents of the SNS as a whole.*

While H1a and H1b are related to the question whether the students would use and value the SNS as the central coordination platform of the class, H2a and H2b focused on the effects of the phase concept and the team building approach as means of teaching presence and as instruments that influence social presence. Our findings indicate that the SNS led to a well-meshed network of relationships among the students from the participating locations and that the development of these relations was fundamentally influenced by the chosen phase concept and team building approach. Also, the SNS was used intensely and continuously throughout all three phases of the setting: preparation phase, production phase and case study phase. Also, as intended, the team managers of the 27 international teams stood out due to their high centrality within the network.

Based on these findings, our future work will now focus on the apparent limitations and gaps of the presented analysis, which we consider to be only a first step:

- Thus far, we did not look at the quality of the connections and interactions between the students. On what issues and in what ways did they communicate and collaborate with the help of the SNS? In addition to a better understanding of the adoption of the SNS, such analysis would also allow us to gain further insights into the social presence that was actually established through the SNS.

- As means of teaching presence we not only developed the described phase concept and team building approach, but also a comprehensive role concept. While we addressed the effects of the assignment of the team manager role in this paper, we did not cover the additional roles of 'editor, blogger & presenter' and 'reviewer' thus far.

- Finally, instructional settings in general and thus also e-learning settings like the Net Economy class require cognitive objectives. We therefore also need to elaborate on the cognitive effects and effectiveness of the described setting in general and the discussed means of teaching presence in particular. This again will require a semantic analysis of the SNS usage.

While being aware of these fundamental additional research needs, we consider both the implementation of the SNS as a social coordination platform and the phase concept with its team building approach to be successful. Besides the value of these results for our own and similar e-learning settings, we see our paper as a contribution that provides evidence for the controllability of SNS as a means of social presence in instructional settings. The paper thus fits into the Community of Inquiry framework that we referred to as the theoretical foundation of our conceptual efforts which demands that social presence needs to be controlled and managed by a teaching presence.

We agree with Garrison (2011) who states that it is unclear at this point whether social media will have a significant role to play in mainstream higher education, but at the same time we feel highly motivated to continue our path of integrating a SNS as a major component of our international cross-location e-learning setting Net Economy. In conclusion, we see good chances for social media to be incorporated in e-learning successfully, if carried out carefully.

References

Anderson, T., Rourke, L., Garrison, D. R., & Archer, W. (2001). Assessing teacher presence in a computer conferencing context. *Journal of Asynchronous Learning Networks, 5*(2), 1–17.

Bastian, M., Heymann, S., & Jacomy, M. *Gephi: An open source software for exploring and manipulating networks.* International AAAI Conference on Weblogs and Social Media.

Biswas, G., Leelawong, K., Schwartz, D., & Vye, N. (2005). Learning by Teaching: A New Agent Paradigm for Educational Software. *Applied Artificial Intelligence, 19*, 363–392.

Boccaletti, S., Latora, V., Moreno, Y., Chavez, M., & Hwang, D. (2006). Complex networks: Structure and dynamics. *Physics reports, 424*(4), 175–308.

Borgatti, S., & Everett, M. (2006). A graph-theoretic perspective on centrality. *Social networks, 28*(4), 466–484.

Boyd, D., & Ellison, N. B. (2007). Social Network Sites: Definition, History, and Scholarship. *Journal of Computer-Mediated Communication, 13*(1-2).

Carmines, E., & Zeller, R. (1979). *Reliability and validity assessment* (Vol. 17): Sage Publications, Inc.

Colazzo, L., Magagnino, F., Molinari, A., & Villa, N. (2008). From e-learning to Social Networking: a Case Study. In C. J. Bonk, M. M. Lee, & T. Reynolds (Eds.), *Proceedings of World Conference on E-Learning in Corporate, Government, Healthcare, and Higher Education 2008* (pp. 670-677). Las Vegas, Nevada, USA: AACE.

Dalsgaard, C. (2008). Social networking sites: Transparency in online education. http://eunis.dk/papers/p41.pdf, Retrieved on July 24, 2012.

Decker, R., Rašković, S., & Brunsiek, K. (2010). Diskriminanzanalyse. *Handbuch der sozialwissenschaftlichen Datenanalyse*, 495–523.

Freeman, L. (1979). Centrality in social networks conceptual clarification. *Social networks, 1*(3), 215–239.

Gabriel, R., Gersch, M., Weber, P., Le, S., & Lehr, C. (2009). Enhancing Professional, Media, and Social Competencies through International Collaborative E-Learning. In T. Bastiaens, J. Dron, & C. Xin (Eds.), *Proceedings of World Conference on E-Learning in Corporate, Government, Healthcare, and Higher Education 2009* (pp. 1248-1255). Vancouver, Canada: AACE.

Garrison, D. R. (2011). *E-learning in the 21st century: A framework for research and practice* (2nd ed.). New York: Routledge.

Garrison, D. R., Anderson, T., & Archer, W. (2001). Critical thinking, cognitive presence and computer conferencing in distance education. *American Journal of of Distance Education, 15*(1), 7–23.

Gersch, M., Lehr, C., & Weber, P. (2011). VIRTUAL COLLABORATIVE LEARNING IN INTERNATIONAL SETTINGS – THE VIRTUAL SEMINAR "NET ECONOMY". In : *5th International Technology, Education and Development Conference, INTED2011 Proceedings* (pp. 5078–5085). IATED.

Hamat, A., Embi, M. A., & Hassan, H. A. (2012). The Use of Social Networking Sites among Malaysian University Students. *International Education Studies, 5*(3), 56–66.

Hartshorne, R., & Ajjan, H. (2009). Examining student decisions to adopt Web 2.0 technologies: theory and empirical tests. *J. Computing in Higher Education, 21*(3), 183–198.

Hu, Y. (2005). Efficient, high-quality force-directed graph drawing. *Mathematica Journal, 10*(1), 37–71.

Liccardi, I., Ounnas, A., Pau, R., Massey, E., Kinnunen, P., Lewthwaite, S., … (2007). The role of social networks in students' learning experiences Annual Joint Conference Integrating Technology into Computer Science Education Dundee, Scotland Workshop Session: Working group reports table of. In *Annual Joint Conference Integrating Technology into Computer Science Education. Workshop Session: Working group reports* (pp. 224–237). Dundee.

Liu, M., Kalk, D., Kinney, L., & Orr, G. (2012). Web 2.0 and Its Use in Higher Education from 2007-2009: A Review of Literature. *International Journal on E-Learning, 11*(2), 153-179.

Mendoza, S. (2009). The Trinity of Community: Google, Facebook and Twitter. In T. Bastiaens, J. Dron, & C. Xin (Eds.), *Proceedings of World Conference on E-Learning in Corporate, Government, Healthcare, and Higher Education 2009* (pp. 3555-3562). Vancouver, Canada: AACE.

O'Donoghue, J., & Warman, L. (2009). Can social networking support student retention? In George Siemens & Catherine Fulford (Eds.), *Proceedings of World Conference on Educational Multimedia, Hypermedia and Telecommunications 2009* (pp. 3011-3015). Honolulu, HI, USA: AACE.

O'Reilly, T. (2005). *What Is Web 2.0? Design Patterns and Business Models for the Next Generation of Software*: O'Reilly Media, Inc.

Oblinger, D., & Oblinger, J. L. (2005). *Educating the net generation*. Boulder, CO: EDUCAUSE.

Roblyer, M. D., McDaniel, M., Webb, M., Herman, J., & Witty, J. V. (2010). Findings on Facebook in higher education: A comparison of college faculty and student uses and perceptions of social networking sites. *The Internet and Higher Education, 13*(3), 134-140.

Safran, C., Helic, D., & Gütl, C. (2007). E-Learning practices and Web 2.0. In *Proceedings of the International Conference on Interactive Computer Aided Learning* (pp. 1–8).

Scott, J. (1988). Social network analysis. *Sociology, 22*(1), 109.

Watts, D., & Strogatz, S. (1998). Collective dynamics of 'small-world'networks. *nature, 393*(6684), 440–442.

10 Aligning Facebook and Twitter with Social Studies Curriculum

Emin Kilinc, Russell T. Evans, Ummugulsum Korkmaz

Introduction

Technology implementation in schools has been extensively studied in the United States for several decades (Becker, 1994; Cuban, 2001; Culp, Honey, & Mandinach, 2003). Technology is seen as a golden key in facilitating technology-enhanced, student-centered teaching environments (Hannafin & Land, 1997). With the expeditious progression of technology, school districts spent millions of dollars to equip classrooms with the belief that technology can improve instruction and engage students (Stobaugh & Tassell, 2011). A recent survey shows that ninety-seven percent of teachers had a computer located in their classroom; however, teachers reported that neither they nor their students used computers in the classroom often (40%) or sometimes (29%) during instruction time (Gray, Thomas & Lewis, 2010).

Technology has become a necessity in schools to convey curriculum material to students. School districts feel that most technology provides students with a unique tool that can offer them a truly enriching learning experience. As social studies classrooms rely on discussions and critical thinking; incorporating technology provides a nice medium for students to interact with one another. While technology seems to provide ample opportunities for students to apply their social studies knowledge, it has not been without its problems. Problems in social studies education stem from how to utilize technology to making lessons more meaningful as students grow into participating citizens.

Teachers have to take on the shared responsibility of properly educating students in regard to online attitudes and behaviors. If teachers do not take the initiative to educate students in this regard, students will not be able to understand that there is a responsibility behind the glow of the Internet. Teachers also have a responsibility for ensuring that students in the social studies classroom are molded into good citizens. Technology assists teachers in making political accessibility possible for students. State and local officials are standing in full support of the future of social studies technology. According to Friedman (2006) these officials are taking this opportunity to really connect with their fellow citizens. These officials want a connection to their electorate because they want to understand the issues people want them to tackle. Friedman (2006) concludes that students that are well aware of these avenues of communication will become better citizens.

There are emerging technologies that can enhance students' classroom experiences along with allowing cultivating them into strong citizens. Social networking tools such as Facebook and Twitter are opening the doors to connecting students across classrooms and around the globe. Social networking tools are defined as the practice of expanding knowledge by making connections with individuals of similar interests (Hayes, Ruchman, & Walker, 2009). Social networking sites are online spaces that can be customized to a large extent by their users, providing space for personal profiles, which users complete in order to make connections with others. Social networking refers to sites such as Facebook, MySpace, and LinkedIn (Gunawerdana et al., 2009). It can be concluded that these social networking tools, facilitate interaction, collaboration and increase attention to the social studies. In fact, more than 55% of all online American youths ages 12–17 use online social networking sites (Pew Internet, 2007). It stands to reason that there is great potential for teachers to build upon the students' existing social network and leverage students' comfort with Web 2.0 technology within their classrooms (Drexler, Baralt, & Dawson, 2008).

Among the social networking outlets, Facebook is now the largest social networking site with a growth rate of 97% just over 2008. On January 18, 2011, The New York Times mentioned that Facebook is the world's largest social network and it announced in July 2010 that it had 500 million users around the world. The infrastructure of Facebook has grown rapidly over the last few years, setting itself apart among its competitors. Technology is evolving at such a rapid pace that the now third ranking site, Twitter, did not even place in the top seven in 2007 (Hayes, Ruschman, and Walker, 2009).

It stands to reason that there is great potential for teachers to build upon the students' existing social network and leverage students' comfort with social networking tools within their classrooms; however due to network security issues and internet safety concern, schools are slow to adopt new technologies. When schools improve their access to technology, the most cited reason for lack of implementation of new technology is lack of professional development (Drexler, Baralt, and Dawson, 2008). Finally, it can be concluded that using social networking tools to increase student engagement in social studies, increases their awareness to solve community and global problems. These tools generally provide students with an open forum in which they can become active citizens.

How to Use Facebook/Twitter in Social Studies Classrooms

Facebook and Twitter are unique pieces of the social networking landscape that offer ample ways to coordinate the social studies classroom. Facebook and Twitter are social networking sites that students can interact with in a number of ways, including inside the classroom, on their mobile devices or from their homes. Facebook and Twitter are tools that students already make use of to connect with friends; therefore, teachers should further exploit this resource. Many districts, however, have attempted to limit Facebook access in schools. Despite this fact, if teachers have the right training in how to align Facebook with their classroom goals, it can be an extremely rewarding experience for both students and teachers.

The current paper includes a number of ways in which Facebook and Twitter can be logically aligned with pre-existing classroom curriculum. The sections that follow cover many of the ideas and suggestions for social studies teachers to make use of in their own classrooms.

Class Projects/Activities

The social studies classroom has many opportunities for class projects and activities. The following are strategies for using Facebook/Twitter that could be used in completing a project in a single class period or spread over multiple class periods.

- Follow Politicians on Facebook/Twitter: Social studies students can keep up with politicians by being their 'fan' on Facebook/Twitter, this will give students the opportunity to report to the class about any range of facts about politicians. Students can discuss where politicians stand on key issues, their platforms and possibly even share media clips with the class.
- Using News Feeds on Facebook: News feeds offer wide spread amount of information, not limited to the students' friends. If students 'fan' or 'like' certain issues/topics they will have a stream of news from those sources. If there are certain topics students can search for (e.g. Industrialization, Cultural Issues of Southwest Asia, etc.) they can find a group that they can follow to gather information for the purpose of reporting to the class. Many of these news feeds offer information that may align historical topics with current events.
- Classroom Poling Systems on Facebook: Facebook has a feature directly on the profile page that allows students/teachers to create polls on various topics. This interactive teaching tool allows students to get to know one another and where they stand on certain issues. This system isn't limited to position questions but instead could also be used in helping students to review material for quizzes/exams.
- News Creation with Facebook/Twitter: Students can use status updates on Facebook/Twitter to create news from chapters they are reading. Students can 'break news' as they cover different parts of the textbook that they are using for class. By allowing them to bring the news of the chapters to Facebook/Twitter, they maintain an open forum in which they can talk about topics raised in class outside of the classroom. Teachers can also moderate the direction of these conversations brought up in news stories.
- Role-Playing on Facebook/Twitter: Students can take on roles or become key people in topics that are discussed in class. Through role-playing students learn how to debate and discuss topics through the eyes of other people. Students can post updates or group/class pages by using parenthesis after their names to show their alternate persona they are trying to emulate.
- Using Facebook Video: Students can narrate their own projects/presentations and allow other students to offer their input/critiques of their work. Facebook video allows students to import video in a number of different formats. Visuals also help many learners in the social studies classroom.
- Social Studies Brainstorm with Facebook/Twitter: Didn't have enough time to finish discussing a topic in class? Allow students to meet online and direct them in a discussion about a topic directly from class. This can save a lot of physical class time in the next class meeting.

Empower Students to Communicate with their Classroom

Bringing communication and dialogues into the classroom is key. Facebook/Twitter offers an excellent way ensure student engagement in learning experiences within the classroom and outside of the classroom. These online opportunities for communication also keep the line of communication between students and teachers open. A foundation of communication outside of the classroom will also make classroom instruction time easier as a level of rapport has already been built with students. These are some ways that Facebook/Twitter can provide those opportunities for direct communication.

- Class Schedule: Sharing the schedule and giving students an online class reference is important in the digital age. If students miss class for any reason, the schedule is accessible to them, allowing them a chance to catch-up or even a chance to get ahead. Important class events can also be planned and scheduled among students and their teacher.
- Class Notes: Sharing notes can be available to students. Notes from class could be downloaded or viewed via Facebook video. This is especially helpful for students absent from class as it makes it easier for numerous students to catch up with the rest of the class without much effort.
- Class Assignments: Social studies class assignments and homework can be posted on Facebook; students can ask teachers questions regarding the assignment. Additionally, they can also connect with other students they might not have formally met in class to help them answer their questions.
- Groups on Facebook: Groups can be created and moderated by teachers. This feature allows different class sections to study together. It provides a centralized place to meet for each of their different classes. Students don't have to 'friend' other classmates or their teacher on Facebook for this to work. Information can easily be shared and communicated with other students through group pages.
- Direct teacher-student communication: Informal contact can be made with teachers through Facebook/Twitter. Students can use this tool to get in touch with teachers throughout the day or in the evening, making communication accessible even if students cannot return to the social studies classroom during the day.
- Forum for Hard-to-Reach Students: Shy/hard-to-reach students who might not feel comfortable talking in the classroom setting can raise questions on Facebook/Twitter. This can make their personal transition of openly communicating in the social studies classroom much less intimidating.
- Class Announcements: Due dates, quizzes, tests, etc. can all be shared via Facebook/Twitter. Students can openly communicate about upcoming events. Additionally, teachers can use this feature to reach all of their class sections regarding last minute announcements/changes in schedules (if needed) with one keystroke.
- Web Share: Students find interesting websites and resources online all the time. Web Share allows students the opportunity to share resources with other students that might take an extremely long time to come-up with on your own. Teachers can save these resources and make them available to other current class sections and future social studies classes. Web Share also enables direct communication among students. This idea is useful on both Facebook/Twitter.

Positive Features of Facebook/Twitter in the Classroom

As already discussed, Facebook/Twitter is a beneficial tool in the classroom. Beyond the benefits there are also some key features of using Facebook/Twitter in the classroom that can be noted in the lesson design.

- Inviting: Facebook/Twitter is equal parts the students and the teachers' tool for the social studies classroom. It does not belong more so to one party over the other, which makes it unique for the classroom experience. This feature alone makes it useful for classroom teachers.
- Informal: The informal nature of Facebook/Twitter is one that makes well-suited for using it in the social studies classroom. Facebook/Twitter allows students to participate in a variety of ways whereas the social studies classroom usually only allows students to participate in a few ways. Through Facebook/Twitter they can not only participate in a variety of ways but also students can access it from any location making it convenient to their schedule.
- Collaboration: Facebook/Twitter sets the stage for students to collaborate with each other. Students are comfortable with Facebook/Twitter and it promotes dialogue among students. This is key when talking

about class projects or group assignments. Collaboration will also make students team players in the social studies classroom.

- Current: Facebook/Twitter are currently two of the most frequented websites on a daily basis and both are in the process of evolving while continuing to grow. For educators, to be on the forefront of a new technology shows students that their teacher is willing to accept this change and bring the classroom into the 21st century. Facebook/Twitter serves as a means to promote student innovation within the framework of the social studies curriculum.
- Student Engagement: Students with the availability of social networking websites like Facebook/Twitter are more likely to stay engaged outside of class. Students can access the class from anywhere allowing them to follow their assignments and lessons, and stay connected with the social studies classroom.
- Responsibility: Along with engagement and level of access comes responsibility. Since this tool is all around them, they have few excuses not be informed about their classwork. Likewise this environment provides educators with the opportunity to teach students personal responsibility regarding Internet sites like Facebook/Twitter.

Conclusion and Tips for Social Studies Teachers

If teachers choose to utilize social networking tools like Facebook and Twitter in their classrooms, teachers need to be aware of their own use on these sites. While both sites offer significant benefits, teachers need to protect their own interests and maintain a professional relationship with their students. Below are some suggestions regarding educators' level of interaction and general tips for use.

- Separate Personal/Professional Facebook/Twitter Account: Maintaining two accounts (personal/professional) accounts for social networking sites is important. This allows elements of your private life to remain private while still allowing students to see their teacher in a professional way. There will be no need for students to transition between school and online interactions, since both will be similar.
- Friend/Follow Students Wisely: Students in both current and previous classes must be treated equally. Students share access to their accounts, thus making it even more important to keep all relationships in check. Educators must monitor privacy settings before engaging with students. Likewise, notify students through instruction to limit your (teacher) access to what you (teacher) can see on their pages (e.g. teachers should not have access to student photo albums). It is important to maintain a professional relationship with students as you would normally in the classroom.
- Lists: Lists provide ways for teachers to stay organized between classes. Teachers can maintain lists on both Facebook/Twitter, which allow them to keep their students organized when it comes to grading and assessing students' level of activity on social-networking sites.
- Facebook/Twitter as a Class Management System: Facebook/Twitter can replace costly class management systems (e.g. Blackboard, WebCT). Teachers don't need to ask their school to purchase license agreements with expensive class management sites; instead, teachers can use free/inexpensive alternatives through social networking tools such as Facebook/Twitter.
- Engage Regularly: It is extremely vital for educators to remain engaged with their classes by posting on a daily bases. These updates will keep students engaged along with keeping their own level of interest/activity at a high level. Teachers must put into social networking sites exactly what they expect out of them.

References

Becker, H. J. (1994). Analysis and trends of school use of new information technologies. Washington, DC: Office of Technology Assessment.

Cuban, L. (2001). Oversold and underused: Computers in the classroom. Cambridge, MA: Harvard University Press.

Culp, K. M., Honey, M., & Mandinach, E. (2003). A retrospective on twenty years of education technology policy. Washington, DC: U.S. Department of Education, Office of Educational Technology.

Drexler, W., Baralt, A., & Dawson, K. (2008). The Teach Web 2.0 Consortium: a tool to promote educational social networking and Web 2.0 use among educators. *Educational Media International, 45*(4), 271-283.

Friedman, A. M. (2006). The internet's potential to affect social studies and democracy. *International Journal of Social Education, 21*(1), 44-58.

Gray, L., Thomas, N., & Lewis, L. (2010). Teachers' use of educational technology in U.S. public schools: 2009 (NCES 2010-040). Washington, DC: National Center for Education Statistics, Institute of Education Sciences, U.S. Department of Education.

Gunawardena, C.N., Hermans, M.B., Sanchez, D., Richmond, C., Bohley, M., & Tuttle, R. (2009). A theoretical framework for building online communities of practice with social networking tools. *Educational Media International, 46*(1), 3-16.

Hayes, T.J., Ruschman, D., & Walker, M.W.(2009) Social networking as an admission tool: A case study in success. *Journal of Marketing for Higher Education, 19*(2), 109-124.

National Council for the Social Studies. (2010). *National curriculum standards for social studies: A framework for teaching, learning, and assessment.* Washington, DC: National Council for the Social Studies.

Stobaugh, R. R., & Tassell, J. L. (2011). Analyzing the degree of technology use occurring pre-service teacher education. . Educational Assessment, Evaluation and Accountability, 23(2), 143-157.

11 CARE: Creating Augmented Reality in Education

Farzana Latif

Introduction

Augmented Reality (AR) combines the 'real' world with that which is 'virtual'. It is considered a sub set of Mixed Reality (Miligram and Kishino, 1994) and is closely tied to Virtual Reality (ibid). Whilst AR is not a new phenomenon, mobile phones are helping to make it an increasingly achievable option in learning, teaching and student services, in terms of time, cost and the technical skills required for development. This has arguably been made possible through powerful operating systems and better hardware (for example, cameras and compasses) on mobile devices, as well as the increased use of such devices. Some AR definitions consider the type of devices used to combine the real and virtual world (Azuma, 1997). Here a broad definition of AR is adopted: "[AR] ... refers to a wide spectrum of technologies that project computer generated materials, such as text, images, and video, onto users' perceptions of the real world." (Yuen et al., 2011, p.120).

The scope of this project is limited to smartphones and tablets (such as the Apple iPad, Samsung Galaxy Tab) running the iOS or Android operating systems and the terms 'mobile phone' and 'mobile device' are used to encompass both of these groups of technologies. Yuen, et al. (2011, p.122) propose that in order to make the most out of mobile AR, devices should include: GPS technology (for location-finding); an accelerometer (to detect device movement); and a digital compass (for direction-finding). For this project it is also necessary for devices to include a rear-facing camera (i.e. a camera on the opposite side to the device's screen). Mobile augmented reality browsers, including Layar (http://www.layar.com), Junaio (http://www.junaio.com), Wikitude (http://www.wikitude.com) and Aurasma (http://www.aurasma.com), utilize these features. They offer functionality such as image recognition (also known as optical tracking) and location based services. These browsers can be installed and used on mobile devices free of charge, although there is sometimes costs involved in accessing content. The features in mobile AR browsers can enrich the student experience, allowing them to connect with a whole host of resources in a context specific manner, supporting experiential learning, and offering a new dimension to traditional methods. The portability of mobile devices offers the ability to take teaching out of the classroom and away from a fixed position, whilst exploiting the fun and excitement that AR brings to an experience. The immersive nature of AR and mobile devices lends itself to pervasive, ubiquitous, learning (Syvänen, 2005).

Cases

The engaging nature of AR is arguably one of the reasons that has led to its increased use in marketing. The 2011 NMC Horizon Report describes its use in education as changing from "gimmick to a bonafide game-changer" (Johnson, et al., 2011, p.16). In order to achieve this there is a need to innovate and identify its relevance in teaching, learning and student services. The cases described below have been identified to demonstrate and establish suitable AR applications as well as to understand their limitations and the amount of development time required to build these applications. Both of these projects offer opportunities to enhance the methods by which students are currently taught. These ideas emerged through close liaison with academic staff.

Case 1: Clinical Skills Lab

Clinical skills are an essential component of healthcare education for trainee nurses; simulated practice is used to orientate students to the clinical environment. Figure 1 shows the setup of a typical clinical skills laboratory.

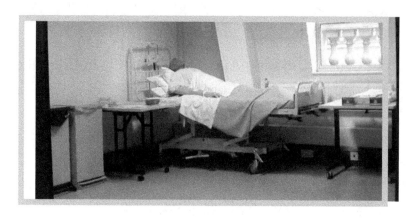

Figure 1: Clinical Skills Laboratory

The first case examines how relevant resources can be overlaid over equipment, dummies and key areas within a clinical skills lab. AR offers the opportunity to overlay environments, such as operating theatre and accident and emergency, making them instantly accessible to students, offering the opportunity to reduce anxiety, increase knowledge and develop skills prior to undertaking clinical placements. The affordance and portability of mobile devices offers an unobtrusive way to interact with environments. It encourages self-directed learning, moving away from a didactic instructor-focused lab. As well as encouraging students to take responsibility for their own learning it offers the potential for these labs to be open for additional hours as fewer teaching staff or technicians will be required to supervise students.

The resources that will be used to overlay objects will primarily be taken from the CETL (Centre for Excellence in Teaching and Learning) website http://www.cetl.org.uk/learning/ which hosts a variety of resources and activities to develop clinical and communication skills. A series of triggers will be set up around a lab to allow students to access key resources. Figure 2 shows how Augmented Reality can be used in a lab.

Triggers (e.g. images) are placed around a lab

Image is viewed using mobile device

Relevant resources are triggered (e.g video)

Figure 2: Example of Augmented Reality in a Lab

The use of AR in this manner could be replicated in other simulated practice environments such as an Ophthalmology lab or a TV production room and is currently being used in museums. The SCARLET (Special Collections using Augmented Reality to Enhance Learning and Teaching) project (http://teamscarlet.wordpress.com/) uses the Junaio AR browser to overlay virtual material on special collections held within the John Ryland library, Manchester, UK. It shares similarities to this case, in that it uses image recognition to identify an artifact rather than using position and direction information.

Case 2: Locality Project

As part of a pre-registration in nursing course, students are allocated to one community of practice in East London. It is very important that students have an appreciation of the culture, history and social composition of the area they are working in. A public health walk, which involves walking around an area while identifying and experiencing public health-related activities and issues, such as the number of fast food outlets, can help identify public health issues (Bryar and Orr; 2012, p. 102). However, students currently struggle with such a task. AR offers the opportunity to reveal aspects of the local area, making them accessible to students from the outset of their course. For this case, the AR solution involves developing a route around East London with key points of interest. When students arrive at different points, they will be able to access key resources and data related to their immediate surroundings. Students will work in groups to encourage collaborative learning, however since the route will be available publically, students have the opportunity to take this route on their own at different times, encouraging self-paced learning. Also key to this project is developing transferable and reflective skills so that students become aware of why particular points of interest have been selected, supporting experiential learning. To encourage these reflection skills, students will be asked to complete tasks after they visit a place, and since students will have a mobile device with them, there is the opportunity for these tasks to include utilising social media such as twitter, taking pictures, creating sound bites and short videos. The resources that will be made available to students and the assigned activities are currently being developed by a team of learning technologists, along with locality and subject experts.

Two projects that share similarities with this case in terms of location tracking use AR browser layer and are being undertaken by The University of Murcia, Spain and The University of Exeter, UK. In the former case students develop a treasure hunt to explore different aspects of Murcia. As part of this activity students complete each others AR treasure hunts (Castaneda, 2012). The latter looks at how scientific virtual data can be overlaid over a countryside that surrounds the University of Exeter (http://blogs.exeter.ac.uk/augmentedreality/about/).

Considerations

As mentioned there are a variety of mobile browsers available to develop AR, they all differ in terms of functionality. Layar, Junaio and Aurasma have been explored, with the latter two currently viewed as more favourable as there are no development costs involved in using them. Whilst the number of people with smartphones and tablets has increased, not all students will have access to this technology, therefore a process for loaning devices to students for use in these projects will be initiated.

In the clinical skills lab, students will be based on University property and the environment is controlled. It is unlikely that in such safe surroundings a mobile device will be stolen, or that defined triggers based on image recognition will be vandalized. For the locality project both are of concern, to help minimize the risk of theft students will be allocated to groups, given guidelines and encouraged to be vigilant. It is important to do this because the immersive nature of AR means that people's attention is focused on the devices and they may be less aware of what is happening around them. Figure 3 shows an image that is significant to one of the key points of interest in the locality project. The pink sticker on the bottom left marks vandalism and could affect whether or not relevant resources are triggered. Additionally, location based services are often only able to pin point locations within a certain range; inaccuracies could make it difficult to find key points.

Figure 3: Vandalism

Evaluation

An evaluation of the students' experience is being planned to identify the effectiveness of both cases both in terms of technology and impact on developing the skills described. To date the technology has been presented and received interest from across the University including academic staff and students from different schools, as well as central services, such as the library and career services.

Conclusion

Whilst AR is not a new phenomenon, the affordances of mobile devices and AR browsers are helping to make it an increasingly achievable option in learning and teaching. The increased use of AR in marketing highlights how engaging the technology is, but in order to exploit it as more than a gimmick, there is a need to innovate and identify its relevance in context-specific environments. The examples considered in this paper offer opportunities to encourage both collaborative and self-directed learning, moving away from a didactic instructor-focused lab. There is an opportunity to use AR in different disciplines and some of these examples have been identified. To ensure equality, it is recommended that arrangements are made to loan devices to students that do not have them.

A variety of AR browsers exist, but differ in terms of functionality. Identifying the most appropriate browser is dependant upon what is trying to be achieved. Using AR in an external environment such as that described for the locality project could encounter issues related to accuracy of location and vandalism to fixed points of interest that act as triggers.

In order to identify the impact of this project an evaluation will be carried out to explore its effectiveness. The results of this evaluation will be shared with the wider community.

References

Azuma, R. T. (1997). A Survey of Augmented Reality. In *Presence: Teleperators and Virtual Environments*, 6(4), 355-385.

Bryar, R. & Orr, J. (2012). The Community Dimension. In K. Lurker, J. Orr & G. A. McHugh (Eds). *Health Visiting: A Rediscovery* (pp 85-118). West Sussex, UK: Blackwell Publishing Ltd.

Castenda, L. (2012) *Exploring Augmented Reality for Non-Formal Learning in a Formal Experience of Educational Discovering*. Retrieved from http://www.pelecon.net/blog-post.php?s=2012-03-11-exploring-augmented-reality-for-nonformal-learning-in-a-formal-experience-of-educational-discovering

Johnson, L., Smith, R., Willis, H., Levine, A., and Haywood, K., (2011). *The 2011 Horizon Report*. Austin, Texas: The New Media Consortium.

Milgram, P. & Kishino, F. (1994). A Taxonomy of Mixed Reality Visual Displays, *IEICE Transactions on Information Systems*, 77(12), 321-9

Syvänen, A., Beale, R., Sharples, M., Ahonen, M., & Lonsdale, P. (2005). Supporting Pervasive Learning Environments: Adaptability and Context Awareness in Mobile Learning. *Proceedings of the IEEE International Workshop on Wireless and Mobile Technologies in Education (WMTE '05)*. IEEE Computer Society, Washington, DC, USA, pp 251-253

Yuen, S., Yaoyuneyong, G. & Johnson, E. (2011). Augmented Reality: An Overview and Five Directions for AR in education. *Journal of Educational Technology Development and Exchange*, 4(1), 119-140.

12 Creating Hybrid Learning Experiences in Robotics: Implications for Supporting Teaching and Learning

Saundra Wever Frerichs, Bradley Barker, Kathy Morgan, Megan Patent-Nygren, Micaela Rezac

Introduction

The Geospatial and Robotics Technologies for the 21st Century (GEAR-Tech-21) program, teaches robotics, global positioning systems (GPS) and geographic information systems (GIS) technologies through hands-on experiential activities designed for youth in grades 5-8. The longer-term goal of the GEAR-Tech-21 program is to prepare youth for twenty-first century careers in science, technology engineering and mathematics (STEM) areas through camps, clubs, robotics competitions and afterschool activities and led by adult volunteers. GEAR-Tech-21 has been made possible through the National Science Foundation Innovative Technology Experiences for Students and Teachers Program (NSF ITEST).

The GEAR-Tech-21 activities use the LEGO® Mindstorms® NXT robotic kit, handheld GPS units, and GIS technology to develop life skills and explore science, engineering, technology, and related careers. Moreover, the project offers 300 hours of activities that are designed to be delivered in informal learning environments such as afterschool and community-based programs for youth. Each activity is aligned to national education standards for science, technology, engineering, and mathematics. The curriculum is also mapped to 21st century workforce skills like teamwork, problem solving, and leadership (Partnership for 21st Century Skills, 2009).

Digital manipulatives such as robotics kits, handheld GPS units, or virtual environments are designed with computational capabilities embedded within the manipulative (Resnick, 1998). As with traditional manipulatives used in classrooms (such as decimal blocks or frog models), digital manipulatives provide opportunities to interact and engage multiple senses, but they can do much more. Digital manipulatives allow youth to collect and interact with data and to construct a personal understanding based upon their experiences (Piaget, 1972). Digital manipulatives can take robotics programs beyond helping youth learn about technology to helping them develop the ability to learn with technology. The GEAR-Tech-21 program has been shown to increase participants' STEM content knowledge as demonstrated on pre-and post-measures (Barker, Grandgenett, Nugent, & Adamchuk, 2010). One of the challenges identified in that study was the need for a systematic professional development program that is designed to train volunteers and professionals to lead GEAR-Tech-21 camps and clubs for a wider audience.

Providing a Digital Learning Experience for Youth

The GEAR-Tech-21 activities have been used to provide a unique learning experience in a variety of contexts. It has successfully been implemented as a classroom-based learning experience, as an afterschool program, in clubs and camps, and by teams participating in educational robotics competitions. The hybrid learning experience that GEAR-Tech-21 has created brings together an on-line curriculum, digital manipulatives and real-world experiences – which have resulted in new roles for learners and instructors. Some attributes that distinguish this new learning experience are:

- Learners are able to work with a partner and progress at their own pace through an activity.
- Learners use the robot to engage in a self-directed cycle of testing, feedback and revision of their computer program with limited input from the instructor.
- Multiple solutions to a given challenge are acceptable.
- Success of the learner is measured by their performance of an activity rather than through testing of knowledge.
- Learners may have more knowledge of how to perform the activity at hand than the instructor.

There are two aspects of this experience that are particular significant in terms of how they impact the role of the volunteer instructor. The first is that many of the volunteers who lead GEAR-Tech-21 activities do not have expertise in computer programming, geospatial technology or robotics, and they often find that the youth they work with have more expertise in using the technologies. The second is that learners are able to progress through an activity at their own pace. This leads to a learning experience that is not always centered on the volunteer instructor, where different groups are working on different tasks.

Shifting Roles for the Volunteer Instructor

As a result of the digital learning experiences in GEAR-Tech-21, the volunteer instructor's role in this project is different from a traditional educator's role of leading and evaluating. The volunteer's role in GEAR-Tech-21 is to facilitate learning by guiding and supporting youth. To be successful, volunteers must be prepared to provide some direct instruction, particularly at the beginning of an activity, *and* be able to guide learners they progress at their own pace through hands-on activities. Volunteers have found that they need to develop skills in asking good questions and facilitating youth developing their own sense of understanding. Troubleshooting strategies are particularly important in encouraging youth to find their own solution rather than relying on volunteer instructors to provide answers when they have difficulties.

The GEAR-Tech-21 program received an NSF ITEST scale-up grant in 2007 and developed a delivery model based as a volunteer instructor led program to serve youth audiences nation-wide. The scale-up plan intends to reach 5,000 youth across the US during the five-year duration of the grant and requires an ever-growing pool of trained volunteers to maintain that level of growth. Actual and projected growth of the project is shown in Figure 1. Figure 1 illustrates the growth of GEAR-Tech-21 camps and clubs from 2007-2011 and projected grown in 2012.

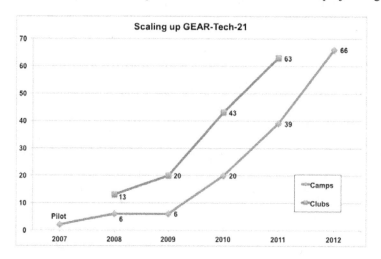

Figure 1: Growth of the GEAR-Tech-21 project over the fiver-year scale up period. Table includes data for 2007-2011 and projected growth for 2012.

Adapting Professional Development to New Roles

Since 2007, the GEAR-Tech-21 team has developed a blended approach to professional development that supports volunteers in developing their skill is guiding youth in STEM activities, and in building their knowledge base and experience in using robotics, GPS and GIS technologies. The pilot GEAR-Tech-21 camps in 2007 were lead by the project's development team, and the initial instructor trainings were conducted as two-day face-to-face hands-on workshops by the same team. To provide continual support to the volunteers who had been trained, additional training opportunities were offered beyond the face-to-face experience.. A blended model of training was implemented to meet the needs of the new and growing pool of instructors. The 4-H SET Volunteer Competencies Training Model in Figure 2 illustrates a blended approach to professional development (Barker, Grandgenett, Nugent, 2009). The team developed printed and on-line resources, and led monthly webinars to support the leaders who had been trained.

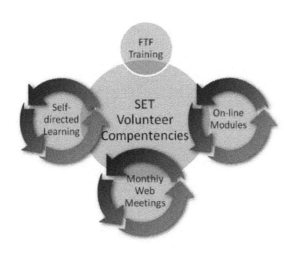

Figure 2: 4-H SET Volunteer Competencies Training Model (Barker, Grandgenett, Nugent, 2009).

In 2010, trainings were held in 10 states across the US and a systematic evaluation was conducted to measure the impact of the trainings. 180 educators across 16 locations in 10 different states that attended training completed a pre- and post-assessment. The instrument has 19 questions, exploring four confidence scales: robotics technology, GPS/GIS technology, use of robotics and GPS/GIS to promote youth learning and motivation, and understanding of STEM to encourage learning and motivation. The survey questions were on a 5-point scale with 1 = strongly disagree and 5 = strongly agree. Overall participants (N=126) rated the training as very good with a mean score of 4.57, SD = 0.57. While most questions (17 out of 19 questions) on the survey had mean scores above 4.0 participants generally felt that the training program was not as effective at providing suggestions for starting a club, camp, or afterschool program (M=3.98, SD=0.87) nor did the training provide effective ideas about raising money to purchase needed robotics and GPS/GIS equipment (M=3.51, SD=1.10). The twelve areas where respondents reported the workshop was most effective are included in Table 1.

Survey Questions	N	Mean	Std. Deviation
The training increased my knowledge and skills in building and programming robots	126	4.70	.58
The training provided concrete activities that I can use with my 4-H club, camp, or afterschool program	124	4.62	.535
Overall, how would you rate this training?	126	4.57	.57
The information presented was relevant to my needs	126	4.56	.56
The training provided a good mix of presentation, discussion, and hands-on activities	125	4.54	.64
The training increased my interest in using robotics technology with my 4-H club, camp, or afterschool program	124	4.53	.70
The design of the training session encouraged a collaborative approach to learning	125	4.53	.55
The trainer displayed an understanding of SET concepts	125	4.52	.60
The training was well organized and executed	125	4.38	.78
The design of the training session reflected careful planning and organization	114	4.33	.76
The training increased my knowledge and skills in the use of GPS/GIS	122	4.29	.74
Formal presentations included in the training session were carried out effectively	125	4.24	.78

Table 1: Results of 2010 evaluation of GEAR-Tech-21 professional development workshops.

As measured by dependent "t" tests, leaders showed significantly improved total confidence in STEM abilities and ability to facilitate youth-based STEM programs. Table 2 includes pre and post mean scores for the total confidence, and subscale scores for a) confidence to perform certain robotics tasks, b) confidence to perform certain GPS/GIS tasks, c) confidence in ability to promote learning of STEM-based knowledge, and d) confidence in facilitating youth based STEM programs. Subscale scores show significant increases in confidence for all four of the subscales as well as the total measure.

Outcome	Pre Mean	Post Mean	t	df	p
Robotics Confidence	54.81	88.56	13.38	130	<.001
GPS/GIS Confidence	47.15	75.25	11.08	124	<.001
Promotion of Learning	49.14	81.67	12.91	124	<.001
SME Facilitation	68.38	90.69	10.81	127	<.001
Total Confidence	54.50	84.11	14.58	130	<.001

Table 2: Overall confidence scores for subscales in 2010 evaluation of GEAR-Tech-21 workshops.

The scale-up plan for the project included a regional trainer model to assist with delivery of face-to-face training for local volunteers that was introduced in 2011. The regional trainers are only responsible for their local area, but strategic selection of regional trainers helped support the continued growth of the project and at the same time, alleviated some of the demands on the core team for face-to-face trainings. They also created a new set of professional development needs. The regional trainers not only need to know how to implement the curriculum in a camp or club program, but also need to develop skills in providing professional development. A train-the-trainer conference was developed to support regional trainers.

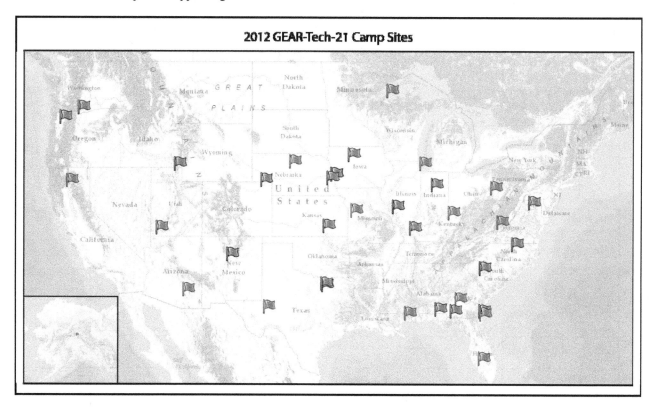

Figure 3: Map illustrates distribution of GEAR-Tech-21 camps across the US in 2012.

Growth of the GEAR-Tech-21 project across the US is illustrated in Figure 3. As the project spreads across the county, program staff and regional trainers are not able to train all prospective camp and club leaders in a face-to-face environment. This led to the development of additional on-line resources, including on-line video-based lessons. In 2012, synchronous and asynchronous on-line courses were added to the professional development repertoire. Today the GEAR-Tech-21 professional development resources include:
- On-line curriculum also available on a DVD

- Helper guides available as a printed book or on-line pdfs for each activity
- Youth notebook available as a printed book or on-line pdfs for each activity
- Face to face trainings led by GEAR-Tech-21 staff, or by regional trainers
- Synchronous and asynchronous on-line course (includes an 8-week course, or 2-day intensive version)
- Use of a project website, Google + Hangouts, Adobe Connect Webinars and other free, current social media
- Just-in-time videos for many of the activities

The aim of the GEAR-Tech-21 program is to prepare youth for twenty-first century careers in STEM by providing hybrid learning experiences utilizing on-line curriculum, digital manipulatives and real-world experience for youth. To prepare volunteer instructors from a variety of backgrounds to lead these learning experiences, the team has also developed a blended approach to professional development. The GEAR-Tech-21 professional development includes many different modes of learning. Digital resources are available on-line as volunteers have a need for professional development and learning can happen when their schedule allows. Synchronous learning experiences (both face to face and on-line) provide a sense of community and support that builds confidence. Printed materials provide yet another level of flexibility and are utilized by volunteers during training and as they lead activities. Evaluation is an important component of the GEAR-Tech-21 project. Pre-and post-assessments are used to measure the impact of professional development efforts. Data from 2010 provides a base-line measure of the effectiveness of face-to-face trainings conducted by the development team. On-going assessments will determine if the Train-the-Trainer model is as effective at increasing volunteers' confidence in robotics, GPS/GIS, and facilitating STEM learning.

For more details about GEAR-Tech-21, visit the project web site. http://4hset.unl.edu

References

Barker, B., Grandgenett, N., & Nugent, G. (2009) A New Model of 4-H Volunteer Development in Science, Engineering, and Technology Programs. Journal of Extension [On-line] 47(2). Available at: http://www.joe.org/joe/2009april/iw4.php

Barker, B., Grandgenett, N., Nugent, G., & Adamchuk, V. (2010) Robots/GPS/GIS, and Programming Technologies: The Power of "Digital Manipulatives" in Youth Extension Experiences. Journal of Extension [On-line] 48(1). Available at: http://www.joe.org/joe/2010february/a7.php

Partnership for 21st Century Skills (2009). *P21 Framework Definitions. Retrieved online http://www.p21.org/overview/skills-framework*

Piaget, J. (1972). The psychology of the child. New York: Basic Books.

Resnick, M. (1998). Technologies for lifelong kindergarten. Educational Technology Research and Development. 46(4), 43-55.

Acknowledgments

This material is based upon work supported by the National Science Foundation under Grant No. ESI-0624591

13 Incorporating Social Oriented Agent and Interactive Simulation in E-learning: Impact on Learning, Perceptions and Experiences to non-Native English Students

Melvin Ballera, Mosbah and Mosbah Mohamed Elssaedi

Introduction

Many years ago, learning English is not mandatory in Libya, making the students today suffered from communication gap among their foreign instructors who tasked to deliver information technology education throughout the country. One of the primary issues is how to deliver lectures that are both difficult to teach and to learn such as automata theory, artificial intelligence, algorithms and other core computer science courses among students. Several educators developed/adapted instructional technologies such as e-learning in delivering learning materials to the students for several years and to fill the gap. However, given the continuous emerging of technology, static e-learning (absence of multimedia, purely textual) becomes outdated and needs to be updated as shown by the series of papers focusing on e-learning development at the university (Ballera & Ziyad, 2010; Ballera & Musa, 2011; and Ballera et. al, 2012). There is a need to develop a new learning environment to lessen the gap in communication and increase the level of understanding and allowing students to navigate their own path of learning, improve knowledge transfer and develop critical thinking.

Face-to-face interaction with pedagogical agent and having an interactive environment capable for motivating the learner to continue the learning process is now common consideration in e-learning development. This situation have motivated the development of a number of theoretical computer simulators as added features of the e-learning module to allow students to "bring to life" many topics that traditionally were presented only mathematically and the use of pedagogical agent that can interact, communicate and help or artificially socialize with the learner (Yurcik et. al, 2002). By adding interactive simulations plus pedagogical agent that can socialize, it is believed that learning becomes enticing and more motivational among learners. Inclusion of interactive simulations will improve learning and develop critical thinking among students who have difficulty in understanding English as medium of instructions. In this paper, we begin by reviewing the literature relevant to pedagogical agents and importance of computer simulations and interactivity. Next, we present our research questions and method of investigating them, then the results and analysis and conclusions.

Review of related Literature

The pedagogical agent literature suggests that agents can serve numerous instructional roles such as tutor, personal assistant, buddy, and counselor and can also serve many functions (Fernely et. al, 2006). Pedagogical agent could enable "increased motivation (Moreno et. al., 2001) increased smoothness of information and communication processes, increased critical thinking and develop problem solving skills (Gulz, 2004). It is just a human-like characters that are included in educational and instructional materials in order to somehow stimulate the learning process (Reategui et. al., 2007). In extending this investigation, Veletsianos et al. (2011) found that pedagogical agents were also expected to socialize and engage with the learner, provide systematic instruction and engender realistic instructional approaches that aid the learning process and support cognitive processing and metacognitive skills. Social interactions and communication to pedagogical agent appear to be positively related to student satisfaction (Aragon, 2003), enjoyment (Berge et. al., 2005) and social immersion (Morton, 2005). Doering et. al (2008) found that learners engaged in multifaceted social dialogue with the agent providing significant increase of learning. According to Kim et. al. (2006) a learner can learn content through interacting with pedagogical agent, who may provide information or encouragement, share menial tasks, or collaborate with the learner. While this literature demonstrates various benefits of social dialogue, few have use this opportunity in developing e-learning of abstracts courses in computer science. Also given the educational settings where communication problem exist, interacting with the agent is not enough. E-learning that merely allows the learner to navigate content, or take an online test, interact with pedagogical agent is often labeled as interactive. This does not meet the criteria of a meaningful interactivity. To fill the gap, interactive simulations and visualization tools should be incorporated in e-learning where a learner can actively explore a simulated system or process to deepen understanding of ambiguous or challenging content (Fulton, 2001).

Interactive simulations and modeling tools are the best examples of complex, meaningful interactivity. Such applications model a real or theoretical system, allowing users to manipulate input variables to change the system behavior and view the results. With such applications, learners can construct and test hypotheses and received feedback as a result of their actions. It is believed by many instructional designers that interactive lessons allows "learning by doing" and arouses interest and generates motivation and provide more engaging experience for the learner (Brookfield, 1986). Interactivity is seen as part of the e-learning system where learners are not passive recipients of information, but engage with material that is responsive to their actions. Interactivity results in deeper learning because learner can hypothesize to test their understanding (Miller, 2009) learn by mistakes (Kolb, 1984) and redoing the process.

In this paper, we have designed an e-learning module that incorporate social-oriented pedagogical agent with interactive simulation environment and investigate its impact on student learning, perceptions, and experiences for non-native English speakers students of computer science. Further, we hypothesize that adding interactive simulations to existing e-learning system with social pedagogical agent will not increases or improve learning outcomes and perceptions of the agent's interactional ability. Specifically, it answers the question: What is the impact of having socially capable agent and interactive simulation in learning and perception and experiences among students?

Methodology

Participants and Materials

Participants were enrolled in Formal Languages and Automata Theory (FLAT), one of the core computer courses where students find it difficult to grasp the concepts due to the abstract formal notations and symbols. The study has been conducted for two semesters at university consisting of 2 groups; The first group uses e-learning with socially oriented pedagogical agent. The agent interject social remarks to help the learner to continue the learning process given a different situation as shown in Table 1. The students participated in the first group were 25. The second group on the other hand uses e-learning module that contains agents similar to group 1 with the addition of interactive simulations during the learning process. There were 25 students participated in group 2. Among the fifty students, there were 6 males and 44 females. The materials used in this study consisted of three tutorials, one pedagogical agent, a demographic profile survey, a pre-test exam, a post-test exam and an open ended interview.

Tutorials

Three tutorials were developed and incorporated to e-learning for the purpose of studying FLAT; deterministic finite automata (DFA), Context Free Grammars (CFG) and Non-Deterministic Finite Automata (NPDA). All topics were abstracts and represented by complex notations and difficult to understand unless given a very good examples. In the first group, the lectures have been presented with the help of agent and minimal human instructor in English instructions while the other group used e-learning that has pedagogical agents, and interactive simulations. The tutorial's contents were expected to be unfamiliar to the students as the study was conducted on the first time each class.

In the first tutorial of FLAT, the deterministic finite automata (DFA) has been used.; usually concepts has been denoted by abstract notations and symbols such as $M = \{\sum, \Gamma, \delta, q_0, F\}$. Fig. 1 shows the abstract equivalent of the Man-Wolf-Goat-Cabbage (MWGC) Problem. Students who usually see such notation have difficulty understanding the matter especially for non-native English speakers. Our experienced showed that students were more attentive if given visualization through interactive simulations, pictures and videos.

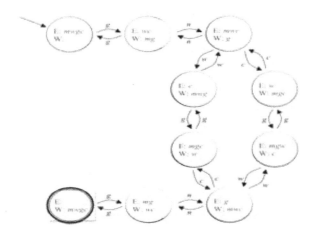

Fig. 1. Abstract Representation of MWGC problem

Fig. 2. The pedagogical agent giving instructions while solving the
MWGC Problem in Interactive Simulations

Figure 2 shows the interactive simulation of the MWGC problem where learner can directly solve by clicking the mouse. Every wrong move, the female agent can interject social statements allowing learner to modify its solution. Agent will continue monitoring the learner's moves until it will reach the final answer.

Similarly second and third tutorial under CFG and NPDA includes interactive simulators where students can try, modify, create program, analyze output, and redo the execution. The agent interject social remarks and help the learner to solve the problem according to given situation. Table 1 shows some social remarks from the agent during the conversation and problem solving of the learners. All social remarks have been pre-programmed and can be activated given some conditions. Example, if the student will not solve the problem in given time, agent will pop some message making the learner to continue the process.

Pedagogical Agent

One animated female agent was used in this study. The agent delivered a lecture verbally using Text-to-Speech technology and explain the simulation while it is being played. Because of the communication gap – the agent will explain the tutorial in a minimal manner and can be interrupted by the learner as s/he chooses too. At the end of the lecture, students were provided with fifteen multiple choice questions. Pedagogical Agent provide verbal response to the question every time the learner clicked the answer and explain if needed. If the answer of the learner is wrong the Agent will socially communicate with the learner and repeat the process. Table 1 summarizes some of the social interjection of the pedagogical agent given a scenario.

Agent Roles	Triggering Scenario	Social Interjections
Personal Assistant	Receptionist Searching for information Schedules Reminders	*"Welcome to e-learning Mr/Ms. "Name"!* *"One moment, Please, I am now searching"* *"I am sorry, information is not available"* *"Here is the information"* *"Your last session was"* *"Exam is set on"*
Tutor/Demonstrator	Tutoring Error Identification Demonstrate	*"I want to show you more"* *"Error occur, please go back"* *"Error has been identified in"* *"Please watch"* *"Allow me to demonstrate"*
Lecturer	Motivational Discussion Question and Answer	*"Continue, excellent"* *"Please, proceed"* *"Wow"* *"I will discuss the matter"* *"Do you have a question*
Advisor Peer/Buddy	Give Suggestion Social Chatting Help	*"Hello, additional example is available"* *"Student X is currently online"* *"Please help me"* *"Need help?"*
Entertainer	Repetitive Reading Time Constraints	*"Seems very hard ah! Would you like to take a break?"* *"Do you feel bored? Here are some tips!"* *"Oh, time lapsed"*

Table 1. Agents Roles and Social Interjections

During tutorials, the pedagogical agent was programmed to communicate with the learner like welcoming, offering help, hints, reinforcing statements, asking questions and provide explanation.
Pre-Survey and Exams

A survey was used to collect (a) demographic information such as gender , age, year level and grade point average, (b) information for knowledge of technology use in education, (c) student perceptions of the agent's interaction ability, and (d) information regarding the use of interactive simulations. Survey responses were combined to form an index measuring computer knowledge of technology use in education (the extent of participants' knowledge of using technology for pedagogical purposes), and an index measuring agents' perceived interaction ability and an index regarding the use of interactive simulations. To determine the internal consistency of survey responses of the above mentioned indices, a Crobach analysis has been used (see equation 1). The Cronbach's alpha is the coefficients of internal reliability, Cronbach values for knowledge of technology is .79 and for the perceived interaction ability indexed at. 72 and index for interactive simulation is .75. Values above .70 are considered satisfactory.

Equation 1

$$\kappa\ Standardized = \frac{K\varpi}{(1 + (K - 1)\varpi)}$$

where K is as above and ϖ the mean of the K (K-1)/2 non-redundant <u>correlation coefficients</u>.

Post-Test Exam and Interview

Participants completed an exam consisting of 15 questions focusing on the three topics presented to them. Five of these questions were recalled information (3 were multiple choice and 2 fill in the blanks) and five problem solving skills with 2 marks each is given. To minimize discrepancies in the exam results, participants were encouraged to leave questions and avoid guessing if they did not know or remember the answer to the questions.

At the end of the exams, participants were invited/interviewed to discuss their experiences in interacting with the pedagogical agents and their views on interactive simulations in the learning process. Participants responses and description, observation will be collected.

Data Analysis

The data informing this study are both quantitative and qualitative. The quantitative data were collected from demographic profile and pre-survey results. In comparing student group performance t-test have been used to measure the perceived interaction ability, increase of learning. Further we use Pearson Correlation Coefficient .(test validity), Cronbach alpha (internal reliability), and learning level (Blooms cognitive level). The qualitative data on the other hand were collected via students description, observation and opinions and then combined to note emerging pattern and to gain understanding of the learner experience. Data will be re-analyzed until saturation has been reached

Results and Analysis

The study's findings are presented under quantitative and qualitative section. The quantitative refer to the demographic profile, perceived interaction ability of the agent, learning of the students and importance of the interactive simulation. The qualitative refers to the saturated responses of the learner based on their quotes and feeling towards the e-learning module.

Quantitative Results

Results indicated no significant effects of the gender (6 males and 44 females), age (mean = 21 and SD=1.17), year level (3rd year) and grade point average (mean=62.68, SD=10.52) and knowledge of computer technology (mean = 4.6, SD= 1.01) These variables do not explain any variations across the two groups. Dependent variables means and standard deviation are shown in Table 2.

The conducted test validity using Pearson Correlation Coefficient shows that there is s strong positive correlation of the exams results with computed $r(23)=.80$, $p<.05$ (critical value=.396) and Crobach internal reliability of .80. T-test indicated that learning outcome differ significantly between the two groups (df = 25, $p<.005$ $t_{computed}=.000015$). In learning dependent variable agent alone have M=10.52 while the SD is 1.55 while agent plus interactive simulation have a M=14.08 with SD = 1.07. According to the study there is also a significant increase of the learning as shown by Blooms cognitive level. Bloom cognitive level revealed that four pattern have emerge with the study with their corresponding average difficulty; Remember (.68) Understanding (.55) Application (.82) and Analyze (.62). In other words students, there is a significant difference of the two groups with regards to learning. The agents with interactive simulations must be adapted in e-learning systems implementation.

Dependent Variable	Group	n	Mean	SD
Learning	*Social Agent*	25	10.52	1.55
	Social Agent + Interactive Simulation	25	14.08	1.07
	Total	50	12.3	2.23
Interaction Ability	*Social Agent*	25	9.6	2.27
	Social Agent + Interactive Simulation	25	14.20	1.07
	Total	50	8.70	1.86

Table 2. Sample size, mean and standard deviation(SD)

With regards to perceived interaction ability of the agents in both group, T-test revealed that difference is statistically significant. The calculated probability is less than .05 (df = 25, $p<.005$ $t_{computed}=.00021$). The agent interaction ability gives a Mean = 9.6 with SD = 2.27 while agent with interactive simulation has Mean of 14.2 with SD of 1.07. Simply stated that, agent with interactive simulation is far better that the agent alone.

Qualitative Analysis

Qualitative analysis generated five themes as shown in Table 3. We presented and described each theme using representative quotes to illustrate our findings and discussed its implications.

Theme
Memorable in a way that we remember the interactive simulation to understand the concepts
Visualization increases understanding since it allows to see theory in practical manner
Dissatisfied with the agent's look, voice, response
Provide informal communication
Very limited because it cannot comprehend different level of students

Table 3. Qualitative Themes

Memorable in a way that we remember the interactive simulation to understand the concepts – Both participants in each group agreed that using the agent plus the used of interactive simulation makes the lessons memorable. The main focus on this theme is the answer of the question "what makes the e-learning memorable ... what's the *reason* that it's memorable?" Jamal says that "The interactive simulation somehow fill the gap of communication problems., since it gives us more time to process data rather than human instructor". Also, Gezala mentioned that "the picture of the agent is beautiful and can communicate well in minimal manner and can guide you step by step in solving problem." Katlon commented further that the "English of the agent is very minimal, I can play several times and then perform by myself without the agent's supervision because I remember the step." Thus, simulations and visualizations tools make it possible for student to bridge experience and remember better the lessons presented to them. It has been observed that students remember the concepts make them actively participate in the classroom learning.

Visualization increases understanding since it allowed us to see theory in practical manner – Turning the abstracts and mathematical concepts into interactive simulations can deepen understanding. Mohamad commented "I understand better the theory with applied simulations because I was able to play and do it by myself how to solve the MWGC problem". Najma on the other hand comment, that "I no longer seek my teacher to repeat and repeat the theory in the board since I can visualize the theory using simulations so I cannot see the angry face of my teacher." Interactive simulations allow students to deepen learning because learners can hypothesize to test their understanding, redo the process, learn by mistakes and develop critical thinking. One student whom we thoroughly observed during tutorial is Sweker; he has difficulty in understanding English and very hesitant to learn the language. Interestingly he commented that " I was able to answer problem given because I was able to relate what I have done and experience during the interactive simulation of the tutorial". Thus the inclusion of interactive simulations in the e-learning improve the quality and outcomes of the tutorials.

Dissatisfied with the agents – Among the 50 students it is very interesting to note that 28 students were able to observe and tell us that the agent has been preprogrammed only and cannot address individual students because of different background and students' cognitive level. Male students further demand for male agents that support them and not a female animated agent. Jamal complained and asked that "Why English accent, why not Filipino or American accent?, I still prefer human teacher". There is also an overwhelming comments that agent's computer generated voice is totally "annoying", "monotonous", "serious" and "non-enthusiastic". Salma, a very good student who know how to write and speak English observed that the quality of the sound is poor and no words emphasis for important words. In general, participants find it difficult to understand but a good substitute and support mechanism for none-native English students.

Provide informal communication – Participants in both groups noted that agent only focus on the dedicated task thus provide efficiency but impersonal. A student who momentarily takes a break can no longer follow the instructions and can cause problems. Informal communication, is implicit, spontaneous multidimensional and diverse. Given our experience, majority of students suffered from short attentive span and spoon feeding, making them lose attention to the tutorial. The agent cannot direct his attention back to the task. Sinosi said, "The agent cannot be interrupted during discussion, so I have to play it again". Also, since the social interjections have been pre-programmed to say words, different students find it difficult to understand. Hawa said "I don't understand, what does it mean?" With this, agents and interactive simulation cause deceptions, and can transmit completely imprecise information that may harm rather help the students.

Very limited because it cannot comprehend different level of students – Diversified students have different level of understanding, some believes that it can aid the learning but cannot support individualization. Agents and interactive simulation is focus on one task and cannot produce more examples among students to understand better the tutorials. Tutorials have limited topics and cannot address the diversified way of teaching. Salma said " agent has a limited communicative skills while interactive simulation is very limited". Another consideration is that different students have different preferences, learning styles, background and difficulty level. Some are fast learners, while others need to be reinforced.

Discussion

This investigation commenced with the following questions: Does agent and the presence of interactive simulation add any benefits to learning? Or, does it hinder learning. How do learners respond to social agents. The answer of these questions raise the implications for the design of online instructional materials and pedagogical agent per se. Empirical results show that there are benefits of incorporating agents and interactive simulations in e-learning systems. Through interactive simulation students were able to do "learning by doing" by allowing themselves to do actual practice in the FLAT simulators and playing games. Comparing the results of the pre-test and post-test it shows that there is significant difference statistically. Simulations and modeling tools are the best examples of complex, meaningful interactivity. Such applications model a real or theoretical system; once incorporated in e-learning, it allows users to manipulate input, change variables, can construct hypothesis and received feedback. Thus, this could be substituted to students who have difficulty in English communication by doing self practice. Inclusion of interactive simulation deepen learning, develop critical thinking and problem solving skills.

The findings of this research shows that with the present of the agent both have advantages and disadvantages. Learners can be motivated and continue the learning process, provided social interjections is minimal. For the first time students who dealt with the tutorials were impressed that agent can communicate with them and a good substitute for human instructor. On the other hand, too much interjections and bombardment of the agents to the learners become irritating and does not reinforce learning process at all. In view with the limited pre-programmed social interjections of the agent, the learner and agents interactivity do not guarantee if it contribute to enhance learning and instructional delivery. Researchers who are interested in exploring social agents should not only consider whether agents contribute to learning gains but also addressed cultural differences, individualization and collaborative aspect of learning process.

The findings of the research also include the meaning and importance of experiences towards agent-based and interactive simulation. Initially the learning environment is enticing, making it memorable for first time users. Some students were dissatisfied due to varied background among learners, limited communicative skills of the agent, few examples, and provide informal communication. Thus making the agent unsettling, distracting and disturbing. This hypothesis could be further examine by future research.

Conclusion

In this paper, we investigate the impact of agent and interactive base e-learning system into students learning, perceptions on interaction ability and learner experiences based on two groups. With regards to learning, results revealed that agent with interactive simulations performed better than agent alone. Blooms cognitive level shows a dramatic increase of learning based on the exams results analysis. Qualitative results illuminated the reasons for findings, indicating that the study is effective and helpful but provide informal communication, limited, memorable, and provide dissatisfaction among diverse learners.

Instructional designer are encouraged further to incorporate interactive simulation that allows "learning by doing" and consider agents to be more intelligent. The development of such environment could serve as bridge among students especially for none-native English speakers. Proper interjection of social remarks should also put into consideration to determine if its help or hinder the learning process. Although social agents and the used of interactive simulation is very effective, the increasing use of pedagogical agents within digital learning environments should still be continuously evaluated and studied including agent roles, proper communication, design per se and further increase of learning, enhanced critical thinking and problem solving skills. The following will be addressed soon in the next paper.

References

Aragon, S. (2003). Creating social presence in online learning environments. New Directions for Adult and Continuing Education, 100, 57–68.

Ballera, M., Omar, A. (2012). Exploring Social Networking Technology and Multiple Pedagogical Agents: How, When and to What Extent they Facilitate Learning in E-Learning System. To be Appeared in the International Conference on Information Communication Technologies in Education (ICICTE 2012). Rhodes Island, Greece.

Ballera, M., Musa, A. (2011). Personlize eLearning System using Three Parameters and Genetic Algorithms – Proceedings of Society for Information Technology & Teacher Education International Conference, -March 7, 2011 (pp 569-574) Nashville, Tennessee, USA

Ballera, M., Ziyad. A. (2010). An Assessment Study and the Design of E-Learning System Strategy in Computer Science Department of Sirte University – appeared in the proceedings of 5th International Conference on Electrical and Electronic Engineering October 23-26 2010, Tripoli, Libya.

Berge, Z. L., Muilenburg, L. Y., (2005). Student barriers to online learning: A factor analytic study. Distance Education, 26(1), 29–48.

Brookfield, S. D. (1986) Understanding and facilitating adult learning. San Francisco: Jossey-Bass. ISBN 1-55542-355-8.

Doering, A., Veletsianos, G., & Yerasimou, T. (2008). Conversational agents and their longitudinal affordances on communication and interaction. Journal of Interactive Learning Research, 19(2), 251–270.

Fulton, K. (2001) WBEC The Power of the Internet for Learning. Report of the Web-Based Education Commission to the President and Congress of the United States. Retrieved on http://www.techknowlogia.org/TKL_Articles / PDF/277.pdf

Gulz, A. (2004). Benefits of virtual characters in computer based learning environments: Claims and evidence. International Journal of Artificial Intelligence in Education, 14, 313–334.

Kim, Y., & Baylor, A. L. (2006). Pedagogical agents as learning companions: The role of agent competency and type of interaction. Educational Technology Research and Development, 54(03), 223-243.

Kolb, David. (1984). Experential Learning: Experience as the source of learning and development. Engelwood Cliffs, NJ. Prentice Hall. ISBN 0-13295-261-0.

Miller, C., Veletsianos, G., & Doering, A. (2009). EnALI: A research and design framework for virtual characters and pedagogical agents. Journal of Educational Computing Research, 41(2), 171–194.

Moreno, R., Mayer, R.E., Spires, H.A., Lester, J. C. (2001) The case for social agency in computer-based teaching: Do students learn more deeply when they interact with animated pedagogical agents. Cognition and Instruction, v. 19, pp 177-213.

Morton, H., Jack, M.A. (2005). Scenario-based spoken interaction with virtual agents. Computer-Assisted Language Learning, v. 18 pp. 171-191.

Reategui, E., Polonia, E., Roland. (2007). The role of animated pedagogical agents in scenario-based language e-learning: a case study. International Conference on Computer Aided Learning (ICL 2007) . September 26-28, Villach, Austria.

Veletsianos, G., Gulz, A., Haake, M., Sjoden, B. (2011). Building a Social Conversational Pedagogical Agent: Design Challenges and Methodological approaches. Conversational Agents and Natural language Interaction: Techniques and Effective Practice (pp. 128-155). IGI Global.

Yurcik, W., Chesnever. C., Cobo, M. (2003). Using Theoretical Computer Simulators for Formal Languages and Automata Theory. Retrived in http://cs.uns.edu.ar/~cic/2003/2003_sigcse.pdf

14 How Virtual Learning Environments Function to Simulate IEP Team Meetings in a Distance Teacher Education Program

Lee L Mason, Nancy Glomb, Peter Blair

Introduction

Simulation training literature suggests that learning through simulations can be an effective method of developing skills and becoming adept at dealing with situations that are likely to occur in the future (Fowler & Pusch, 2010; Ward, Williams, & Hancock, 2006). For pre-service teachers enrolled in a distance degree program, however, geographic barriers may prohibit the use of simulation training to develop certain skills such as the collaborative development of individualized education programs. The use of multi-user virtual environments appears to be a promising medium for connecting pre-service teachers located hundreds of miles apart and facilitating the use of educational simulations to teach the special education eligibility and IEP process.

The purpose of this study was to analyze the function of simulated IEP team meetings in a multi-user virtual environment for distance undergraduate students learning to become special education teachers. Given the diverse range of individual characteristics and background experiences of each participant in this research, the extent to which these setting events differentially affected the IEP team simulations was also considered. From this research, a better understanding of the benefits and challenges of learning in multi-user virtual environments was sought.

In essence, this study was a functional assessment of the use of a multi-user virtual environment to simulate IEP team meetings for distance undergraduate students enrolled in a mild/moderate special education teacher preparation program. Through qualitative methods, antecedent → behavior → consequence (ABC) data, the experiences and perceptions of distance undergraduate students participating in these virtual simulations were explored.

Theoretical Framework

Although rarely used in qualitative research (Day, 1969; Hayes, Blackledge, Barnes-Holmes, 2001), applied behavior analysis (ABA) provides an appropriate theoretical framework for the current study. The use of ABA as a framework narrows the focus qualitative results to Skinner's three-term contingency. In other words, particular attention will be paid to the antecedent stimuli eliciting participant behavior, participants' descriptions of the behaviors in which they engage, and the contingencies controlling the behaviors. Functional behavior assessment (FBA) is the process of identifying environmental events associated with a particular behavior, which allow behavior analysts to generate hypotheses about behavioral function. This information is then used to alter important environmental antecedents or consequences to produce desired behavior change. In the current study, an ABA theoretical framework allowed for a functional assessment of pre-service special education teachers learning to conduct IEP team meetings through virtual simulations. Specifically, this included: (a) A description of IEP behaviors, including classes or sequences of behaviors that commonly occur together; (b) identification of the events, times, and situations that predict when these behaviors occur across the full range of IEP team meetings; and (c) identification of the consequences that maintain the behaviors, and therefore the use of virtual simulations to train pre-service special education teachers. In other words, the theoretical framework of applied behavior analysis allowed for the examination of what functions IEP team simulations appear to serve for teacher trainees.

Procedures

This study employed a multiple case study design. Case studies are often used in educational research to describe an event or process in its natural setting. Yin (2009) defines a case study as "an empirical inquiry which investigates a phenomenon within its real-life context when the boundaries between phenomenon and context are not clearly evident and in which multiple sources of evidence are used" (p. 18). For the purpose of the current research, case study analysis allowed for an investigation into the use of virtual simulations (contemporary phenomenon) to train pre-service special education teachers to conduct IEP team meetings (real-life context).

Furthermore, multiple case study analysis allows for a systematic examination of differences across cases, and incorporation of multiple sources of data (Eisenhardt, 1989; Yin, 2009). Thus, multiple case designs may provide more robust and compelling evidence than individual case studies or other research designs.

Data Collection

A variety of data collection methods were utilized to achieve a clearer understanding of distance students' perspectives of virtual simulation. Data were collected through interviews and observations, as well as document and record analysis of individual assignments, data compiled by the IEP team, and overall rating of each meeting by the course instructor. Information gathering involved both direct and indirect methods. Direct observation involved observing and recording the pre-service teacher's behavior and events in the environment while the behavior was occurring. Indirect methods included record reviews, interviews or questionnaires, and tools to assess the broader physical or social environment. While indirect methods provided a great deal of descriptive information, direct methods were used to confirm ideas about the variables affecting behavior.

Findings

Findings were primarily identified through participant interviews and substantiated through observations and document review. Figure 1 displays an outline of how the findings are presented in this section. Each participant's individual background (Tier 1) is first presented to provide the context for her actions as part of the IEP team (Tier 2). Finally, the collective experiences of all participants are presented to juxtapose the contingencies maintaining these behaviors, and the verbal statements constructed by each participant (Tier 3).

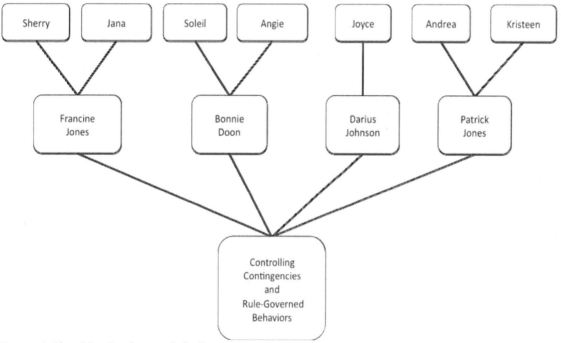

Figure 1: Tiered levels of research findings.

This section describes the contextual variables specific to each of the seven participants in the study. Specifically, these are the antecedent stimuli that prompted each participant to become a special education teacher, and earn her degree through the distance mild/moderate special education program at Utah State University. Although handing out the course assignment was clearly the catalyst that ultimately brought about the target behavior (simulating IEP team meetings in a virtual environment), there were many other controlling factors for each pre-service special education teacher that directly or indirectly affected her behavior. Since simulating IEP team meetings was an assignment for a class that was part of a program in which the participants enrolled, focus was shifted to the antecedent variables responsible for each participant joining the distance mild/moderate program.

Additionally, the motivating operations, or value- and behavior-altering effects of the controlling contingencies, specific to each individual were discussed. In other words, becoming a special education teacher has always been an option for the participants, through either face-to-face classes are offered at state and private universities, or online classes taken from home. Even Utah State University's distance mild/moderate special education program has existed in some form since 1996. So what changed in the lives of each participant to suddenly make becoming a special education teacher more valuable, prompting them to join the 2010 distance cohort?

Due to the magnitude of the unit of analysis, each participant was asked to identify the variables she found most relevant. Four themes emerged across the verbal statements of all participants. These are: (a) Background in special education, (b) Distance program selection, (c) Familiarity with technology, and (d) Prior experience with IEPs. To get a better understanding of the environmental context (both the motivating operations and antecedent stimuli) unique to each pre-service teacher, the findings are stratified by both participant and theme.

Four themes emerged from the discussion of antecedent variables responsible for students enrolling in the mild/moderate distance special education program, and, ultimately, taking part in IEP team simulations. The first was each teacher trainee's background in special education (see Figure 2). The participants all had prior involvement with people with disabilities, but their experience in special education ranged from none (i.e., Soleil) to several years (i.e., Sherry and Angie).

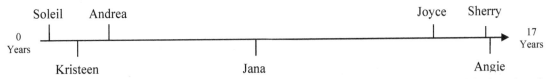

Figure 2: Continuum representing the relative duration of each participant's tenure in special education, from shortest (left) to longest (right).

Six of the seven pre-service special education teachers who participated in this research had worked as a para-educator in a special education classroom before deciding to become a special education teacher. Five of the respondents were working in a special education classroom while taking special education coursework. Many of the participants who were working in special education felt they were already fulfilling the requirements of a special education teacher on a day-to-day basis. This prompted them to enroll in a degree completion and certification program, which, upon completion, would allow them to take over their own special education classrooms.

Length of time in special education did not necessarily correlate with previous experience conducting IEP team meetings, however (see Figure 3).

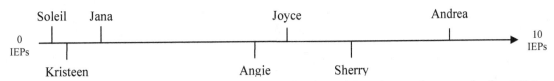

Figure 3: Continuum representing the relative amount of each participant's experience conducting IEP team meetings, from least (left) to most (right).

Although Andrea had spent only a couple of years in the classroom, she was the only participant on an emergency authorization to teach special education. Therefore, she had conducted several IEPs over the prior school year. Sherry had also once conducted an IEP meeting in the past. She stated, however, that she merely filled in for another teacher, and thus considered herself inexperienced in regard to IEP development. The mere fact that she had sat in on and participated in a meeting however, ranked her second amongst the other participants, who had either no previous IEP experience, or had only been able to observe throughout the meetings.

The self-reported level of each participant's level of proficiency with technology was also examined as an antecedent variable (see Figure 4).

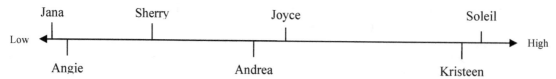

Figure 4: Continuum representing the relative level of each participant's technological proficiency, from low (left) to high (right).

The pre-service special education teachers in this research spoke of a variety of technologies they used in either school or personal settings. Soleil and Kristeen were by far the most competent with the use of technology. Others, like Joyce and Sherry, used Skype to communicate with family members on a regular basis. Jana and Angie expressed the least amount of familiarity with technology.

Additionally, participants cited a variety of reason for choosing to enroll in a distance undergraduate degree and teacher certification program, rather than a more traditional on-campus, face-to-face program. Figure 5 shows the relative distance from each participant to both Utah State University's main campus in Logan, as well as each other.

Figure 5: Continuum representing the relative distance between participants, as well as their proximity to the main campus, from furthest (left) to closest (right).

These were primarily due to ties to the local community that prevented them from relocating. Those who lived close enough to commute – Angie, Jana, Sherry, and Soleil – cited other barriers, such as dangerous driving conditions and difficulty parking on campus.

Although it was not identified as a theme from participant responses, each participant's age was also taken into account (see Figure 6).

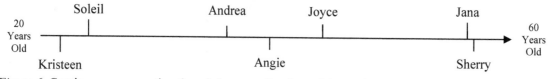

Figure 6: Continuum representing the relative age of each participant, from youngest (left) to oldest (right).

All of the pre-service special education teachers were old enough (i.e., out of high-school long enough) to be considered nontraditional undergraduate students. However, their age ranges varied from the early 20's (Kristeen and Soleil) to the senior level (Sherry and Jana). Further information about the nontraditional characteristics of each participant can be found in Table 1.

Table 1
Nontraditional status of participants.

	Andrea	Angie	Jana	Joyce	Kristeen	Sherry	Soleil
Delayed Enrollment	X	X	X	X	X	X	X
Employed Full-Time	X	X	X	X		X	
Financially Independent	X	X	X	X		X	X
Dependents	X	X		X			X
Single Parent	X						
Nontraditional Status	High	High	Moderate	High	Minimal	Moderate	Moderate

Three of the pre-service special education teachers were classified as highly nontraditional (four or more characteristics). Another three of the participants fell into the moderately nontraditional category (two or three characteristics). Only Kristeen fit the minimally nontraditional standard of just one nontraditional characteristic. It should be noted, however, that these are not fixed classifications, and it is possible to become more or less nontraditional throughout one's school career.

Conclusions

This study addressed questions related to the application of simulation training in distance education coursework for pre-service teachers. This study investigated perceptions of the methods employed, provided theoretical underpinnings, and promoted the development of theoretically sound virtual simulations. Specifically, the findings of this study addressed the efficacy of conducting educational simulations in multi-user virtual environments. Thus, the intent of this study provided a descriptive explanation for better understanding the context of virtual educational simulations from the participants' perspectives.

References

Day, W. F. (1969). Radical behaviorism in reconciliation with phenomenology. *Journal of the Experimental Analysis of Behavior, 12,* 315-328.

Eisenhardt, K. M. (1989). Building theories from case study research. *The Academy of Management Review, 14,* 532-550.

Fowler, S. M., & Pusch, M. D. (2010). Intercultural simulation games: A review (of the United States and beyond). *Simulation & Gaming, 41,* 94-115.

Hayes, S. C., Blackledge, J. T., & Barnes-Holmes, D. (2001). Language and cognition: Constructing an alternative approach within the behavioral tradition. In S. C. Hayes, D. Barnes-Holmes, & B. Roche (Eds.), *Relational frame theory: A post-Skinnerian account of human language and cognition.* New York: Plenum.

Ward, P., Williams, A. M., & Hancock, P. A. (2006). Simulation for performance and training. In: K.A. Ericsson, N. Charness, P.J. Feltovich, and R.R. Hoffman (Eds.) *The Cambridge Handbook of Expertise and Expert Performance.* New York, Cambridge University Press.

Yin, R. K. (2009). *Case study research: Design and methods* (4th Ed). Thousand Oaks, CA: Sage Publications, Inc.

Acknowledgements

This research was supported in part by the United States Department of Education, Office of Special Education Programs (OSEP), award #H325T070039.

15 English Collocation Learning through Corpus Data; On-line Concordance and Statistical Information

Hiroshi Ohtake, Nobuyuki Fujita, Takeshi Kawamoto, Yoshihiro Ugawa, Brian Morren, Hiroaki Takeuchi, Masataka Takekoshi, Shuji Kaneko

Introduction

In this paper, we focus on a number of erroneous collocation patterns that frequently appear in the English academic writing of Japanese medical researchers. Such expressions tend to differ from the commonly accepted forms used by native English speakers in academic discourse (Ohtake & Morren, 2001, 2003). As a result, the writing of Japanese researchers is marred by a certain number of unnatural word collocation patterns that do not conform to conventional practices in academic writing. This is unfortunate, since using an inappropriate word or expression may lead to imprecision in their writing and distract from the meaning they wish to convey (Howarth, 1998).

While Japanese researchers may have a reasonable grasp of grammar, it appears that they have an imperfect understanding of lexical relations. In particular, they have difficulty in selecting a preferred linguistic sequence from a number of grammatically acceptable alternatives (Pawley & Syder, 1983). In this regard, it has been found that words are not independent entities but co-dependent constituents of lexical phrases. Thus, their particular meaning is not constant and unchanging but determined by their relations with other words in the text and by their syntactic and collocational patterns (Beheydt, 1987; Leffa, 1998; Partington, 1998; Stubbs, 2001). Words can therefore be seen to interact with each other not in random clusters but in a clearly principled way (Sinclair, 1991; Willis, 1990). They thereby form predictable and stable combinations that consistently occur in fixed linguistic patterns in conventional academic discourse.

In spite of this, many Japanese researchers seem unaware of a word's natural collocations, resulting in a number of inappropriate expressions such as 'a *low possibility* of membrane destruction,' 'a *high possibility* of benign tumor.' This may be due to a combination of negative transfer from their first language, overgeneralization of grammatical rules, and a lack of exposure to multiple examples of natural academic English usage. It is therefore necessary for Japanese researchers to become more sensitive to the full range of potential meanings of particular words in their various patterns of use if they are to avoid difficulties or errors in choosing the appropriate sense of a word in their academic writing (Biber & Conrad, 2001; Hunston & Francis, 1998).

Collocation Problems

To investigate English collocation problems found in academic papers written by Japanese researchers, we compiled a corpus consisting of English abstracts published in Japan (J-Corpus) and then compared word collocation patterns with those in the Life Science Dictionary Corpus (LSD Corpus) that contains approximately 90,000,000 words collected from life science related research papers published in internationally circulated academic journals. To adjust for the size difference between the two corpora, we also referred to a downscaled version of the LSD Corpus (LSDmini Corpus) whenever necessary.

Table 1 shows an overview of the three corpora. The LSD Corpus contains about 90,000,000 words, the LSDmini 11,120,652 words, and the J-Corpus 11,120,553 words. Each corpus consists of English abstracts published in life science related academic journals. The J-Corpus contains English sentences produced exclusively by Japanese researchers and is therefore meant to be used as a learner corpus.

Corpus Name	Abstracts	Tokens	Types
LSD Corpus (English as the first language)	429,644	89,447,341	387,436
LSDmini Corpus		11,120,652	150,178
J-Corpus (English as a foreign language)	55,973	11,120,553	96,266

LSD: Life Science Dictionary J: Japanese
LSDmini: approximately one ninth of the LSD Corpus
Token: the total number of words   Type: the number of different words

Table 1: Overview of the LSD Corpus, LSDmini Corpus and J-Corpus

To gain insight into the collocation patterns produced by the Japanese researchers, we examined collocates of the English word *similar*. Table 2 shows the statistical data concerning what adverb appears immediately before *similar* in the J-Corpus and the LSDmini Corpus. A close look at Table 2 reveals distinct differences between the two corpora with respect to words modifying *similar*. First, even though the most frequently used adverb is *very* in both corpora, this is followed by *almost* in the J-Corpus, and *structurally* in the LSDmini. As shown in Figure 1, the concordance lines clearly show how Japanese researchers have a preference for using *almost* to modify *similar*. Conversely, the adverb *almost* does not appear in the LSDmini Corpus since it does not usually collocate with *similar* in natural English. Many Japanese learners have therefore failed to grasp that the adverb *almost* should not be used immediately before the word *similar*. The erroneous expression *almost similar* may stem from negative transfer from their first language or failure to fully understand the core meaning of *similar*. The concordance lines in Figure 2 show that *almost* is commonly used immediately before *identical*. To avoid producing these kinds of collocation errors, Japanese researchers should be encouraged to engage in collocation learning based on language corpora.

Secondly, Table 2 shows that the third most frequently used adverb in the J-Corpus, *quite*, is listed as tenth in the LSDmini corpus with only 18 occurrences, which indicates that *quite similar* is not such a preferred expression in academic English writing. Instead, *highly* is used relatively often in the LSDmini Corpus, while it is less commonly used in the J-Corpus. Thirdly, Table 2 also indicates that in the native corpus, *more* and *most* are among the top five collocates and they are the preferred modifiers for *similar*, while in the J-Corpus, *most* is not often used and *more* does not feature in the list at all. This may indicate that when native speakers of English use *similar* in their academic writing, they tend to refer to the comparative degree of the similarity.

Table 3 shows that *almost* is one of the top five collocates of *identical* both in the J-Corpus and the LSDmini Corpus. However, the occurrence of *almost* in the LSDmini Corpus is far less frequent than that of *nearly*, while it is the most frequently used adverb in the J-Corpus. This may indicate that the heavy dependence on this particular adverb is due to the learners' tendency to overuse familiar terms. To raise learners' collocational competence, therefore, it is desirable for them to choose from among the preferred word patterns listed in the corpus rather than depend on a familiar single word or expression that would be collocationally inappropriate.

Rank	1st Left Word (J-Corpus)	Occurrence 4,101	1st Left Word (LSDmini)	Occurrence 8,365
1	very	118	very	274
2	**almost**	**67**	structurally	90
3	quite	64	highly	61
4	qualitatively	17	most	56
5	essentially	14	more	55
6	most	14	remarkably	53
7	closely	13	strikingly	44
8	morphologically	10	qualitatively	22
9	basically	9	functionally	19
10	highly	8	quite	18

Table 2: Top ten adverbs frequently occurring immediately before *similar*

Rank	1st Left Word (J-Corpus)	Occurrence 769	1st Left Word (LSDmini)	Occurrence 1,786
1	almost	80	nearly	120
2	essentially	13	virtually	58
3	nearly	10	almost	51
4	completely	8	essentially	39
5	virtually	6	otherwise	14

Table 3: Top five adverbs frequently occurring immediately before *identical*

```
702                                  Almost similar resistant patterns were seen to S
703                               An almost similar circadian rhythm of enzyme activi
704 e modified Mark IV operation and almost similar anti-reflux effects between both
705 changed for last two decades and almost similar to those of patients with ovarian
706 rmacokinetics of rizatriptan are almost similar between Japanese and other races,
707   bone marrow, megakaryocytes are almost similar in behavior to those in the splee
708 ffect on the pulmonary shunt are almost similar in both groups.
709 ndings in the present family are almost similar to those seen in "adult-onset aut
710 n in umbilical cord blood became almost similar to that of maternal blood at abou
711             15 kD peptide behaved almost similar to PPDs both in the DTH skin reac
```

Figure 1: Excerpt from the concordance for *similar* in the J-Corpus (Erroneous Collocation)

```
266                                  Almost identical porA loci were present in four
267 L mutant shows that it adopts an almost identical conformation with that of the w
268          Alterations within an almost identical copy gene, the centromeric surv
269 , the folding-rate constants are almost identical for the three proteins and clos
270 d -1 ribosomal frameshifting are almost identical from yeast to humans.
271 ree resulting 4D-QSAR models are almost identical in form, and all suggest three
272 nt strains of C. perfringens are almost identical in sequence and biochemical pro
273               The spectra are almost identical to each other and closely corre
274 n two different regions that are almost identical to Escherichia coli K-12 chromo
275 weakly binding PABG fragment are almost identical to those measured in the comple
```

Figure 2: Excerpt from the concordance for *identical* in the LSDmini Corpus (Common Collocation)

Collocation Learning System

As we have shown in the previous section, it is not unusual for English collocation errors to be found in academic papers written by Japanese researchers. In this respect, the system developed by the LSD Project (http://lsd.pharm.kyoto-u.ac.jp) should assist learners in gaining information about how a given English word is actually used in academic writing. In this system, information on word concordances and collocations of English words can be instantly accessed retrieved on-line dictionary. All learners have to do is enter a target word in a word window and press the button. Concordance lines will then appear and with another click of the mouse learners can gain statistical information about common collocates for the target word. Figures 3, 4, and 5 show how learners can take advantage of the system and what kind of output they can derive from this system. In this way, it is possible for learners to acquire a deeper understanding of collocations that cannot be gained by knowledge of grammar alone. This may therefore be of particular benefit to Japanese researchers who have problems in word selection and ultimately lead to a reduction in the number of infelicitous English expressions in their academic writing.

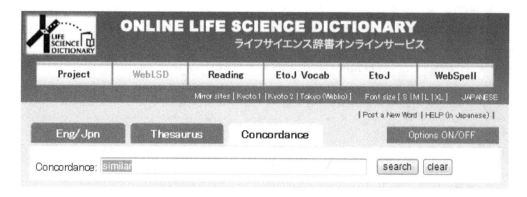

Figure 3: Input window for a target word

```
481 al discrimination tasks activate highly similar aspects of the anterior cingulate
482                            Six are highly similar to their Manduca sexta orthologs
483   of the PP2A phosphatase complex highly similar to Arabidopsis thaliana FASS/TONN
484 , especially when discriminating highly similar stimuli.
485 al reciprocity: (i) they exerted highly similar antimicrobial pH optima and spect
486              Alignment of highly similar UpxYs led to the identification o
487 with and without 11q loss showed highly similar transcriptomic profiles.
488    topologies and PG binding sites highly similar to those of their well-characteri
489 1a mRNA is 1/10 the level of the highly similar SREBP-1c, demonstrated that only
490    Coenzyme B(12) is used by two highly similar radical enzymes, which catalyze c
491 ontent (microarray) analysis was highly similar to their relatedness determined o
```

Figure 4: Excerpt from the concordance for *similar*

Query: similar   No. of hits: 53280   Corpus: LifeSci2008.txt

2nd left		1st left		1st right		2nd right	
a	1827	a	6688	to	20108	that	5843
and	1215	were	4175	in	3232	the	4873
to	1205	was	3263	results	1164	those	4107
is	1203	is	2580	for	870	of	3209
are	1129	are	1946	levels	577	in	2075
that	1102	very	1777	effects	531	were	1478

Figure 5: Excerpt from the collocation statistics for *similar*

CONCLUSION

The above sampling of particular word collocations illustrates how these words are actually used by native English speakers in academic discourse. Although there may at times be a certain degree of variation in their choice of collocates for a given word, the usage tendency can be clearly seen when examining the examples of a word's collocational behavior as exemplified in the LSD corpus. This may thereby offer Japanese researchers a more reliable insight into the unwritten rules of word usages that are not included in the definitions and explanations given in dictionaries or grammar books.

Certainly, for learners to become more proficient writers, they need to acquire more information on which words typically co-occur and the contexts in which certain words may be used (Weinert, 1995; Wray & Perkins, 2000). In this regard, research on language acquisition has shown that lexical items need to be encountered in various types of context in order to more fully appreciate their various meaning senses and how they behave in extended discourse (Laufer, 1990; Schmitt, 1997). Such intensive exposure to regular patterns of language use may therefore provide a better understanding of how such words are bound together with other words, leading to greater clarity of expression. In this respect, the use of corpora and concordance techniques may be a valuable resource in uncovering the syntactic and collocational properties of words and the specific meanings they convey in differing contexts. In particular, they may offer more accessible information on collocations and on the selection restrictions that govern them. Such techniques may therefore raise the awareness of Japanese researchers so that they become more sensitive to the ways in which words combine with other words and help them avoid collocational incongruities in their academic writing.

References

Beheydt, L. 1987. The semantization of vocabulary in foreign language learning. *System,* 15(1): 55-67.

Biber, D., & Conrad, S. 2001. Quantitative corpus-based research: Much more than bean counting. *TESOL Quarterly, 35(2),* pp. 331-336.

Howarth, P. 1998. Phraseology and second language proficiency. *Applied Linguistics, 19(1),* pp. 24-44.

Hunston, S., & Francis, G. 1998. Verbs observed: A corpus-driven pedagogic grammar. *Applied Linguistics, 19 (1),* pp. 45-72.

Kawamoto, T. & Ohtake, H., 2007. *Life Science Collocation with English Sample Sentences and Japanese Translations.* Yodosha, Tokyo, Japan.

Laufer, B. 1990. Ease and difficulty in vocabulary learning: Some teaching implications. *Foreign Language Annals, 23 (2),* pp. 147-155.

Leffa, V. J. 1998. Textual constraints in L2 lexical disambiguation. *System,* 26: 183-194. Life Science Dictionary Project: http://lsd.pharm.kyoto-u.ac.jp/ja/

Ohtake, H. and Morren, B. 2001. A corpus study of lexical semantics in medical English. *Studia Humana et Naturalia,* 35: 15-45.

Ohtake, H. and Morren, B. 2003. Corpus evidence on English collocational patterns in scientific writing: Implications for effective writing development. *Studia Humana et Naturalia,* 37: 41-61.

Partington, A. 1998. *Patterns and Meanings: Using Corpora for English Language Research and Teaching.* John Benjamins: Amsterdam.

Pawley, A. and Syder, F. H. 1983. Two puzzles for linguistic theory: Nativelike selection and nativelike fluency. In J. C. Richards and R. W. Schmidt (Eds.), *Language and Communication,* pp. 191-227. Longman: London.

PubMed: http://www.ncbi.nlm.nih.gov/entrez/query.fcgi?db=PubMed

Schmitt, N. 1997. Vocabulary learning strategies. In N. Schmitt & M. McCarthy (Eds.), Vocabulary: *Description, Acquisition, and Pedagogy,* (pp. 199-227). Cambridge: Cambridge University Press.

Schmitt N, (2000) *Vocabulary in Language Teaching.* Cambridge University Press.

Sinclair, J. M. 1991. *Corpus, Concordance, Collocation.* Oxford University Press: Oxford.

Sinclair, J. M. 1997. Corpus evidence in language description. In A. Wichmann, S.

Stubbs, M. 2001. *Words and Phrases: Corpus Studies of Lexical Semantics.* Blackwell: Oxford UK: Malden, MA, USA.

Weinert, R. 1995. The role of formulaic language in second language acquisition: A review. *Applied Linguistics,* 16: 180-205.

Willis, D. 1990. *The Lexical Syllabus.* Harper: New York; Collins: London.

Wray, A. and Perkins, M. 2000. The functions of formulaic language: An integrated model. *Language and Communication,* 20: 1-28.